Christopher J. H. Wright

Knowing
the Holy Spirit

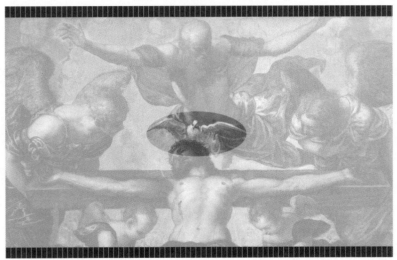

Through the
Old Testament

IVP Academic

An imprint of InterVarsity Press
Downers Grove, Illinois

InterVarsity Press
P.O. Box 1400, Downers Grove, IL 60515-1426
World Wide Web: www.ivpress.com
E-mail: email@ivpress.com

InterVarsity Press® is the book-publishing division of InterVarsity Christian Fellowship/USA®, a student movement
active on campus at hundreds of universities, colleges and schools of nursing in the United States of America, and a
member movement of the International Fellowship of Evangelical Students. For information about local and regional
activities, write Public Relations Dept., InterVarsity Christian Fellowship/USA, 6400 Schroeder Rd., P.O. Box 7895,
Madison, WI 53707-7895, or visit the IVCF website at <www.intervarsity.org>.

All Scripture quotations, unless otherwise indicated, are taken from the Holy Bible, New International Version®.
NIV®. Copyright ©1973, 1978, 1984 by International Bible Society. Used by permission of Zondervan Publishing
House. All rights reserved.

Every effort has been made to obtain permission for quoted material. Any omissions will be rectified in future
printings.

Design: Cindy Kiple
Images: Alinari/Art Resource, NY

ISBN-10: 0-8308-2591-6
ISBN-13: 978-0-8308-2591-2

Printed in the United States of America ∞

Library of Congress Cataloging-in-Publication Data

Wright, Christopher J. H., 1947-
    Knowing the Holy Spirit through the Old Testament / Christopher
J. H. Wright.
      p. cm.
    Includes bibliographical references and indexes.
    ISBN-13: 978-0-8303-2591-2 (pbk.: alk. paper)
    ISBN-10: 0-8303-2591-6 (pbk.: alk. paper)
    1. Holy Spirit—Biblical teaching. 2. Bible. O.T.—Theology
    1. Title.
    BS1199.S69W75 2006
    231'.3—dc22
                                2006020867

P	18	17	16	15	14	13	12	11	10	9	8	7	6	5	4	3	2	1
Y	21	20	19	18	17	16	15	14	13	12	11	10	09	08	07	06		

FOR

HELENA AND BENJAMIN

Contents

Preface

When I told people that I had been invited by the organizers of the New Horizon convention in Northern Ireland in August 2004 to deliver a series of five Bible expositions on the theme of "The Spirit of God in the Old Testament," some wondered if I could find enough to fill one talk, never mind five—such is the widespread lack of awareness among many Christian people of the identity, presence and impact of the Spirit of God in the Bible before Pentecost. It's not that they don't believe he existed before Pentecost. They believe in the Trinity, after all. It's just that they have never noticed how extensive a role the Spirit actually plays in those centuries before Christ. Of course, it could be that they just never read the Old Testament, but let's be charitable.

Even for myself, however, when I got down to the preparation of those five addresses, I discovered there was far more than my first impressions. Some research in concordances and Bible software quickly brought up references I had never noticed before, and as the list grew to fill several pages, it was clear I could not confine the series to just five texts. So I grouped my findings into five major themes, under the titles that now form the chapters of this book. As I came to the end of the series that summer in Northern Ireland, many people came up to share their surprise that they had never realized just how much there was about the Holy Spirit in the Old Testament, and the idea for this book was born.

Some years ago I wrote a book called *Knowing Jesus Through the Old Testament*. It was born out of the conviction that Jesus only makes sense in the light of the Scriptures that shaped his identity and mission, just as the Old Testament itself only makes sense in the light of the Christ who fulfills it. This book reflects a comparable conviction. The Holy Spirit whom we meet in such power in the New Testament—whether in the ministry of Jesus, or the narrative of Acts, or the theology of Paul—is none other than the Spirit of the Lord God of Israel in the Old Testament. So if we want to have a fully biblical understanding of the Holy Spirit, as well as a biblically informed and biblically evaluated experience of his presence and power in our lives, then we need the Old Testament too.

These chapters, then, do not offer another manual on what it means to be sanctified by the Holy Spirit, or how to be filled with the Holy Spirit, or how to exercise the gifts of the Spirit, or how to bear the fruit of the Spirit—all vitally important topics in the teaching of the New Testament on Christian discipleship. What this book does is to ask us to consider that if these are the things we truly seek, do we really know the one from whom we expect to receive them? He is the Spirit who breathed in creation and sustains all life on earth. He is the Spirit who empowered the mighty acts of those who served God over many generations. He is the Spirit who spoke through the prophets, inspiring their commitment to speak the truth and to stand for justice. He is the Spirit who anointed the kings, and ultimately anointed Christ the Servant-King. And he is the Spirit through whom the whole creation will finally be renewed in, through and for Christ. Do we know him? Do we know what we ask for when we ask to receive him? We could not know him clearly apart from Christ and the

New Testament. But we can know him in all his mighty, biblical, divine fullness only through the Old Testament also.

I would like to thank Norman Sinclair and all the rest of the New Horizon team for the invitation to deliver those five addresses on such a subject. The preparation was a blessing to me, just as I pray that this book, which follows the content of the addresses much as they were delivered, with some modification and expansion, especially in the last two chapters, will be one to its readers.

Each new generation is a testimony to the Holy Spirit as "the Lord and giver of life," so this book is dedicated to the next generation of our family in the lives of our first two grandchildren.

Chris Wright

1

The Creating Spirit

The Spirit of God, relegated by some people to his grand entrance on the day of Pentecost, actually appears in the second verse of the Bible:

> In the beginning God created the heavens and the earth. Now the earth was formless and empty, darkness was over the surface of the deep, and the Spirit of God was hovering over the waters. (Gen 1:1-2)

Beginning here, rightly, at the beginning, we shall think first of the Spirit and the *universe*—hovering and speaking. Second, we shall observe the Spirit and the *earth*—sustaining and renewing. Third, we shall consider the Spirit and *human beings*—breathing and leaving. And finally we shall look forward to the Spirit and the *new creation*—groaning and birthing.

HOVERING AND SPEAKING: THE SPIRIT AND THE UNIVERSE

Genesis 1:1, the opening verse of the Bible, makes the fundamental affirmation on which our whole biblical worldview is built. The one living God created everything that we see around, above and beneath us. The whole universe exists because God made it.

The second verse goes on to give us our first picture of creation in its earliest stage—a picture of chaos and darkness. That indeed is how one Bible translation puts it. So does an old Christian hymn:

> Thou, Whose almighty Word
> Chaos and darkness heard
> And took their flight.[1]

The stuff of creation is there, but it has not yet been shaped to the world we now know. But the Spirit of God is there too. Here for the first time also we meet the suggestive range of meaning that the Hebrew word *ruakh* can have. Some translations speak of "the wind of God," or "a mighty wind," blowing over the waters. *Ruakh* can indeed mean wind, and also breath—things that are unseen, but very powerful in their effects. However, almost certainly the writer is speaking of the Spirit of God, in the more personal sense, for he speaks of the Spirit "hovering over the waters" (not "hoovering over the waters," as an international student who was reading the lesson at a service at All Nations Christian College some years ago earnestly asserted). Wind blows; it does not "hover." So we are not just being told that it was a bit windy back at the beginning. Rather we are being told that the powerful Spirit of God was hovering, poised for action. The word "hovering" in Hebrew is used of an eagle hovering in the sky, poised, alert and watchful, ready for instant action to catch its fledglings. In Deuteronomy 32:11 it is a metaphor for God watching over his people.

The action comes in Genesis 1:3, when God spoke into the darkness. There is a close link throughout the Bible between the Spirit and the word of God. It is closest when the word *ruakh* is used alongside the word *neshama*, which also means breath. Either or both together can speak of the powerful, creating, breathing *word* of God. That is what comes into action in this verse.

---

[1]John Marriott, "Thou, Whose Almighty Word," 1813.

Job links together God's power, wisdom, breath, hand and "whisper" in all the great works of creation. These words are all used in a great parallel cooperation:

By his power he churned up the sea;
   by his wisdom he cut Rahab[2] to pieces.
By his breath the skies became fair;
   his hand pierced the gliding serpent.
And these are but the outer fringe of his works;
   how faint the whisper we hear of him!
Who then can understand the thunder of his power?
   (Job 26:12-14)

The Israelites of the Old Testament thought about God as Creator, not only in the teaching of Genesis but also in their worship. Psalm 33 includes a powerful reflection on God as Creator, and the role of his word and his breath in creation. It does not use the word *ruakh*, but comes very close in speaking of God's breath and word together, for these are certainly connected with God's Spirit.

The psalm begins by celebrating the transforming power of the word of God. In Psalm 33:4-5, we hear language that comes from the great exodus deliverance, when God had brought Israel out of the injustice and oppression of their slavery in Egypt, and proved his faithful love to them.

For the word of the LORD is right and true;
   he is faithful in all he does.
The LORD loves righteousness and justice;
   the earth is full of his unfailing love. (Ps 33:4-5)

---

[2]"Rahab" was an ancient mythological name for the great serpent that was thought to inhabit the ocean. Job is here using pictorial language to speak of God's power over the seas and his ability to subdue all forces that might oppose him.

The psalmist affirms that God's word is always like that. It deals in what is right and true, faithful and just, and ultimately fills the earth (not just Israel) with God's love. We need to notice that the psalmist is not just talking about "God" in a general sense, but specifically about the LORD. When this word appears in capital letters as it does in our English Bibles, it is translating the Hebrew personal name of God—Yahweh (or Jehovah in older translations). It is the word of *Yahweh* (not the word of any other god) that is right and true. It is the faithfulness, justice and love of *Yahweh* (not any other god) that will fill the earth.

This is a great vision of the transforming power of the word of this God, embracing the whole earth in its scope. But is it not also grandiose and idealistic? How can the word of the God of a little nation like Israel be a word for the whole earth? The answer comes from Psalm 33:6-9. It is because Yahweh, whom Israel knew as their national redeemer, is also the universal Creator. He is the God of Genesis as well as the God of Exodus. The God of Israel is able to transform the world because he is the Creator of the world. So our anticipation of what he will be able to do in the future is firmly based on our knowledge of what he has already done through his word in the past.

So, in Psalm 33:6-9 the psalmist echoes the great creation narrative by combining the word of the LORD with the breath of his mouth (which as we have seen is closely linked to his Spirit, as in Psalm 104:29-30) and also by combining the great created realities in the same order as Genesis 1—the heavens, the waters and the earth. The psalmist is almost certainly reflecting on that creation narrative and the role of Spirit and word of God in it.

> By the word of the LORD were the heavens made,
>   their starry host by the breath of his mouth.

He gathers the waters of the sea into jars;
>   he puts the deep into storehouses.
Let all the earth fear the LORD;
>   let all the people of the world revere him.
For he spoke, and it came to be;
>   he commanded, and it stood firm. (Ps 33:6-9)

By including all these three great orders of creation—the sky, the sea and the earth—the psalmist challenges our fallen human tendency to turn any or all of them into things we worship in place of their Creator. By implication he also challenges whole worldviews that spring from such idolatries.

- **The heavens (Ps 33:6).** The heavens and all the stars were made by God. But in the surrounding nations the heavenly bodies were very powerful gods. The sun was a major god in Babylon and Egypt. In stark contrast, the account of creation in Genesis 1 did not even name the sun, but simply describes it as the greater of the two big lights that God made and put in the sky! Likewise, the stars were commonly considered deities that controlled human destinies. But Genesis lists them almost as if they were just a divine afterthought: "he also made the stars" (Gen 1:16). The stars? They are not gods! They are just something else that God "also made." Isaiah 40:26 engages in the same kind of unmasking of any divine claims that others might submit for the starry hosts.

  So there is no place, then, in the thinking of this psalm for astrology—that very ancient practice that amazingly survives to this day. The heavenly bodies, far from being deities from which you can get some clue about the present or future, are themselves only created objects that were called into existence by the word of the Lord.

- **The sea (Ps 33:7).** In Canaanite mythology the sea was also a powerful god (called Yamm). The sea was associated with chaotic power and evil. As we saw above, this myth is reflected in Job and elsewhere with the concept of Yahweh's victory over the great deep. But in Genesis the great deep is itself the creation of the Lord God. And here in this psalm, far from something to be afraid of, the sea is put in a very diminutive perspective. The oceans? God's got them in a jam jar. They are just another of the great storehouse of wonders that he made by his creative word.

  So there is no place in this psalmist's thinking for the kind of dualism that pits a good god against an evil one or sees an endless cosmic struggle between chaos and order. The living God has all things, including the oceans, under his control.

- **The earth (Ps 33:8-9).** Canaanites also had a god for the earth. It was especially the role of Baal, the son of El, to provide the fertility of the soil and the animals. So they invested greatly in the so-called fertility cults to ensure health and wealth, through sympathetic religious placation of the gods of the earth. Today various kinds of new spirituality often involve attributing divine status to the earth, as a mother goddess figure, or simply as a cosmic divine life force, with which we need to establish harmony.

  On the contrary, says our psalmist, the earth itself is the creation of God. He simply spoke it into existence with a word of command. So, far from us needing to pay any homage to the earth, the earth itself and all its inhabitants are summoned to pay proper honor to their Creator.

All of these great realities, then, are the effect of the divine word, the work of the same Creator Spirit of God, the product of the breath of his mouth. Our worldview must take this into account. We may (or we may not) like to have a strong emphasis on the Holy Spirit in our ministry or in our particular Christian tradition or in our own personal devotion. But have we included this dimension within our biblical understanding of who the Holy Spirit is and what he has done? The Spirit is the one through whom the living God spoke the universe into existence and brought light, order and fullness to the world we now inhabit. He is, as the Nicene Creed puts it, "the Holy Spirit, the Lord and giver of life."

SUSTAINING AND RENEWING: THE SPIRIT AND THE EARTH

Old Testament Israelites did not spend a lot of time wondering about how the world *began*, except that it began by God's say-so. Once they had affirmed that in Genesis 1—2, enough seemed to have been said. But they did reflect often, and with great wonder, on how the world is continuously *sustained*, restored and rejuvenated. Every day you wake up—it is still there! Which is very reassuring. And just as importantly, the seasons come and go, year in and year out. There is a vast regularity about the whole system of the earth, which the human race has observed for countless generations. And again, the Israelites recognized the hand of their God in that amazing process. So did other nations, of course. All great civilizations have attributed natural processes to whatever gods they worship. The Canaanites had a rich mythology of gods and goddesses through which they explained the cycle of seasons and the annual need for rain and sun and fertility. One major Canaanite myth told of the great battle between Baal (god of life and fertility) and Moth (god of death). Initially Baal is slain (just as the season of growth and fertility comes to an end). But then, with the help of his consort, Asherah, he is brought back from the grave to life again and so the seasonal cycle can continue.

But for the Israelites, life could not be parcelled out to different gods in that way. All life on earth is sustained by the Spirit of God— from the lowliest fish to the most powerful human being. They not only worshiped one God only—their covenant God, Yahweh; they also affirmed that Yahweh alone was God. "You were shown these things," said Moses to the Israelites, speaking of the exodus and their encounter with God at Sinai, "so that you might know that Yahweh is God . . . in heaven above and on the earth beneath; there is no other" (Deut 4:35, 39, my translation). For that reason, therefore, they understood that all life on earth is sustained and renewed by the Spirit of the one living God—from grass-roots level (literally) to the human pinnacle of creation. If it were not for the life-sustaining Spirit of God, life would be instantly extinct, dead in the dust.

> If it were [God's] intention
> and he withdrew his spirit and breath,
> all mankind would perish together
> and man would return to the dust. (Job 34:14-15)

Psalm 104 is a beautiful psalm of creation, celebrating the sheer magnificence of all that God has made. After listing the many wonders, climaxing in human life itself, the psalmist pauses in amazement:

> How many are your works, O LORD!
> In wisdom you made them all;
> the earth is full of your creatures. (Ps 104:24)

Then he goes on from considering the work of God as Creator, to the way God sustains and provides for all he has made. There is no place here for Deism—the belief that once God had created the cosmos, he stepped back and let it run without any personal involvement on his part, like an unwinding clock. God, in the Hebrew world of thought and worship, is not distant and remote from the natural world. On the contrary, God is actively present in sustaining everything that lives and breathes on his planet. And it is precisely through his Spirit that he does this:

> These all look to you
>   to give them their food at the proper time.
> When you give it to them,
>   they gather it up;
> when you open your hand,
>   they are satisfied with good things.
> When you hide your face,
>   they are terrified;
> when you take away their breath,
>   they die and return to the dust.
> When you send your Spirit,
>   they are created,
>   and you renew the face of the earth. (Ps 104:27-30)

So the Creator Spirit is also the provider Spirit. Or, to put it more formally, in this psalm we have moved from the doctrine of creation to the doctrine of providence. God not only brings all things into existence, he also sustains all things by his power. Day by day, season by season, year by year, from age to age, the Spirit of God is there, sustaining and renewing the earth. God the Creator, God the provider—both are truths that the Bible links with the Holy Spirit.

This great truth was also affirmed by Jesus, not about the Holy Spirit directly, but about our heavenly Father. It is God himself, Jesus reminded us, who clothes the grass of the field, and adorns the lilies with their beauty. It is God who feeds the ravens, and knows when a sparrow falls to earth (Mt 6:25-34). Jesus saw in these truths (which of course he learned from his Scriptures—what we call the Old Testament), a great encouragement to personal faith. If your Father God cares so much about even the smallest items in his vast creation, how much more does he care for you—so trust him! Like the psalmist, Jesus knew that if God is everywhere present through his Spirit in the whole of creation, you can never get lost from God (Ps 139:7). So the truth of the universal sustaining, providing, caring role of the Spirit of God in creation is a heart-warming reassurance of our personal security and of provision for our practical needs. If God's Spirit cares in this way for the whole creation, he can certainly manage to care for you. That is a wonderful thought, and we need to hold on to it in faith and confidence.

But although the Old Testament believers could draw the same personal conclusions, it is still very important to note that they affirmed this truth *for its own sake*. God, through his Spirit, has created and continuously sustains all that exists. And he does so for creation's own sake and for God's own glory. And we are part of that. It's not that we say "God cares for me, oh, and by the way he also cares for the rest of creation," but, "God cares for creation, and amazingly, he cares for me too." Similarly, although we often talk about how we are to "care for the environment," it is actually the other way round. It is the environment that cares for us! The "environment," as we lamely call it, is God's creation into which he has put us. And if he did not continuously sustain and renew it, we would not long survive within it. The world we live in, then, is not only the product of the Spirit of God through his almighty word in creation, but it is also the arena of his constant presence, surveillance and sustenance.

And furthermore, God actively loves all that he has made. Psalm 145 echoes the creational language of Psalm 104. It moves from the observation of God's providence in nature to the affirmation of his universal love for all that he has made. The word *all* or *every* (the same word in Hebrew) occurs sixteen times in this one psalm—stressing the limitless universality of God's love as Creator and provider. Not just all the *people*, but *everything* he has made.

> The eyes of all look to you,
>> and you give them their food at the proper time.
> You open your hand
>> and satisfy the desires of every living thing.
> The LORD is righteous in all his ways
>> and loving toward all he has made. (Ps 145:15-17)

So far we have seen that the living God whom Israel knew as Yahweh, their LORD God, is the Creator, sustainer, provider and lover of the whole of creation. And in all these roles, the Spirit of God was and is active. Where does this lead us?

If we long for a deeper experience of the Spirit of God, what exactly are we looking for? It will not mean merely enjoying more spectacular exhibitions of his alleged presence, or exercising more and more of the gifts associated with the Spirit in the New Testament. There are many ways, of course, in which such deeper experience of God's Spirit will affect us (not least in bearing more of the fruit of the Spirit in more Christlike character). But one thing it will certainly do, if we take these Scriptures seriously, is to drive us to a more balanced biblical worldview in which we stand in awe and wonder at the relationship between God and the whole of creation, and take it seriously. It is sad that so many Christians, though claiming to know God and to be filled with his Spirit, pay so little attention to this founda-

tional biblical truth. Or perhaps they treat it as no more than that—
a kind of invisible foundation that they take for granted and think no
more about. "God made the world? Great, what's next?" Whereas, of
course, both in ancient times and today, this is a startlingly aggressive
affirmation, in the context of all kinds of rival claims—religious or
secular.

Or they may be under the sway of a peculiarly negative attitude to
the physical world, thinking that only that which is "spiritual" really
counts at all (which is usually further confined to getting your soul to
heaven when you die, along with as many others as you can take with
you through evangelism). The physical world is either just the dispens-
able stage on which that spiritual drama takes place for the moment;
or worse, it is under some kind of cosmic demolition order just waiting
to be carried out before we can all relocate gratefully to heaven.

Against all such minimizing and trivializing popular viewpoints,
the Bible affirms creation, affirms the whole of creation, and affirms
that the whole of God, including his Spirit, is involved in its origin,
sustenance and future. Our God is the God of the whole creation. He
made it, he sustains it, and he loves it. Such a holistic worldview af-
fects many things, but at least the following two:

1. Science
Science is another of God's great gifts to humanity. Science had its
origin in the biblical worldview that the universe is a rational unity
that can be understood because the consistency of its laws and processes comes from the mind of the one who created it. However, as
modern western science has developed, it tends now toward a dog-
matic naturalism—the view that the material realm is all there is.
Thus, any idea of a divine intelligence behind the origin and structure of the universe or of a divine purpose for which it exists and

to which history is leading is ruled out as fanciful or wishful dreaming.

Against such a mindset, the biblical teaching on creation and providence affirms that the universe is not just a meaningless product of expanding energy. The earth is not just a self-sustaining biosystem. Nature is not just there for human use and exploitation. No, in all that happens, including what we (rightly but insufficiently) call "natural processes," God is actively involved through his Spirit. Indeed the whole of creation in all its fullness is intimately linked to the glory of God—that is, to his reality, his substance, his intrinsic "God-ness." For, as Isaiah heard the heavenly creatures proclaiming, "The whole earth is full of his glory"—or as it could be more literally translated, "The fullness of the earth is his glory." That is, it is not that the earth is like some kind of empty bucket which gets filled up with God's glory. No, the fullness of the earth *is* that glory. The glory of the living God is (at least in part) constituted by the incredible diversity and plenitude of this great living organism we call planet Earth. So also the psalmist, having affirmed the renewing power of the Spirit of God, goes on,

> May the glory of the LORD endure forever;
> may the LORD rejoice in his works. (Ps 104:31)

2. Ecology

If all life on earth is sustained by God, and loved by God, then there are more ways of grieving the Holy Spirit than just lack of personal sanctification. Of course we are aware of all kinds of personal ways in which we can grieve or quench the Holy Spirit in our lives. But here is another way that we have never perhaps thought of as we should. I am constantly surprised at how may Christians have no interest in ecological issues or even in Christian efforts to care for creation through dedicated and scientifically well-accredited conservation work. They know about such things as destruction of habitats, draining of wetlands, burning of forests, pollution of the atmosphere, rivers, and oceans, global warming, loss of species, etc. But they care little, or only in a perfunctory way. Worse, some Christians manage so to distort their view of the future that they have a kind of theology of obliteration. If the whole earth is destined to destruction, they argue, why bother caring for it now. Use it up as fast as we can, before it all goes up in smoke.

And yet they say they believe the Bible, the same Bible that tells us that the earth was made by God the Father, is sustained by God the Spirit and will be the inheritance of God the Son; the same Bible that tells us that God loves all he has made, that the Spirit gives life to all and that God has reconciled all things to himself through the blood of Christ on the cross. And yet they manage to treat this marvelous creation of God with callous contempt—in practice if not in their conscious attitudes.

Surely, we have to protest against such attitudes, especially when they are held by Christians, and challenge ourselves and others to recognize that willful or careless destruction of any part of the good earth God has given us grieves the Holy Spirit who is its Creator and sustainer.

BREATHING AND LEAVING: THE SPIRIT AND HUMANITY

So far we have considered Genesis 1:1-2, along with Psalm 33, relating the Spirit of God to the whole universe. Then we narrowed our focus to the earth itself and enjoyed Psalm 104's portrait of the sustaining and renewing power of the Spirit in all of nature. Now we come to the work of the Spirit of God as Creator particularly in relation to human beings:

> The LORD God formed the human from the dust of the ground[3]
> and breathed into his nostrils the breath of life, and the human
> became a living creature. (Gen 2:7, my translation)

This is a famous verse, but greatly misunderstood, so we have to
deal with that misunderstanding before we can grasp its positive
message. Traditionally and popularly it has been assumed to be a
description of God breathing an immortal soul into Adam, as that
which distinguishes people from animals. The soul, then, is
thought to be something that humans have that animals do not possess, and this verse describes how and when we got it. This view
owed a lot to the older KJV translation of the final phrase, "man became a living soul." However, this will not stand up to careful ex-
amination of the text. We must look at the two phrases—"breath of
life" and "living creature."

"Breath of life" cannot mean an immortal human soul that is distinct from the animals, because the exact same words have already
been used in Genesis 1:30 to describe all animals and birds that live
and breathe on the ground or in the air. The phrase is used again with
the same inclusive sense in Genesis 6:17. It refers simply to the common life of all animals (like mammals) that breathe.

Similarly, the phrase "living creature" is not at all unique to human
beings. It has already been used three times in chapter one (Gen 1:20,
24, 28) to describe the rest of the animal creation, and will be used

---

[3]The first Hebrew word here is *ha'adam*; the second, translated "ground," is *ha'adamah*. It is
clear that the two are related. The human creature is an earth creature—the same connection
that can be seen in the way the word *human* is derived from the Latin word *humus*, which
means "soil." This is why I have translated *ha'adam* as "the human," rather than "man" or even
"Adam." The text is not referring here either to the distinct masculine gender (the distinction
of genders is the focus of the latter part of the story), nor to the named individual, but to the
human being as a distinct species and the unique relationship that God establishes as they are
formed.

again in that way in the flood narrative (Gen 7:4). All humans and animals have this in common: that they are "living creatures." In fact, the word here translated "creature" is indeed the same word that is sometimes translated "soul" (nephesh), but it is not something that human beings uniquely possess. In fact, it is not something that is "possessed" at all. It is what we are, along with other living creatures made by God. God made all living creatures, including us human ones.

So Genesis 2:7 is not telling us how man got his soul. But it is certainly saying something very significant and positive about human life in relation to God. In fact, the point of the verse is not to distinguish us from animals, but to connect us with God. For the words "God breathed into his nostrils" speak of tender, personal intimacy. It is of course a figure of speech (since God does not have literal physical breath). But it is a phrase which, from other contexts, would certainly indicate the presence of the Spirit of God, who can also be called the breath of God (e.g. in Ezek 37:9-10, 14).

As human beings, we are creatures who, like all other mammals, have the breath of life. But we are also uniquely created in God's own image and with special tender intimacy, enlivened with the breath of God. And it is this work of the Spirit in human life that generates all that makes human life so special. Job reflects on this connection between God's Spirit (or breath) and human life and capacity in several places.

> As long as I have life within me,
>   the breath of God in my nostrils,
> my lips will not speak wickedness. (Job 27:3-4)

> But it is the spirit in a man,
>   the breath of the Almighty, that gives him understanding.
>   (Job 32:8)

> The Spirit of God has made me;
>   the breath of the Almighty gives me life. (Job 33:4)

But, as the Genesis story proceeds from this tender creation of human life in intimate relation to God, we come to the horror story of Genesis 3. We sinned. We rebelled. We disobeyed God, choosing to believe a lie, trust ourselves and reject the moral authority of our Creator. And the result was the sentence of death.

Genesis 6:3 makes an interesting comment on the state of affairs that exists because of human sin, and connects it with God's Spirit. We needn't go into detail on Genesis 6:1-2, since there are many different views on what it is describing, except to say that it seems to be talking about some serious transgression of the boundaries between the realms of heaven and earth. But the effect was that God acts to curtail the length of normal human life.

> My Spirit will not remain in the human being forever, for he is flesh. His days shall be limited to a hundred and twenty years. (Gen 6:3, my translation)

Flesh here, in contrast to *spirit*, means "mortal." The point is that human beings do not possess "natural immortality." We live as long as we are given life by God's Spirit. So, yes, all human life is energized by the Spirit of God, in the sense that we are alive and breathing in God's world. But all human life is also mortal. We live only as long as that Spirit remains. When God withdraws that Spirit, we revert to what we are—flesh; and we return to what we are made from—dust. This is the same reality that Psalm 104:29-30 affirms about all animate life on earth, and it is echoed even more bluntly in Ecclesiastes' poetic reflection on human death as the moment when,

> the dust returns to the ground it came from,
> and the spirit returns to God who gave it. (Eccles 12:7)

So the paradox of the relationship between the Spirit of God and human life on earth in the Old Testament is this. On the one hand we have the breath of life—i.e. physical life, the gift of God, which we share with all other living creatures on the planet. But on the other hand we are spiritually dead in our rebellion against God and destined to die in the end when that life-giving Spirit leaves—as destined to die physically as we are already dead spiritually. Hence the paradoxical title of this section—"breathing and leaving." Life and breath are the gift of God's Spirit. But when the Spirit leaves, breathing stops and our mortality asserts itself.

Is there then any hope for us? Is there any hope for creatures like us who have the gift of life through the Spirit of God and yet live under the sentence of death, knowing that the Spirit of God will not remain in us forever in our mortality? Yes indeed, as we shall see in later chapters, and especially when we come to the New Testament. God promised, even in the Old Testament, to give us new life, new hearts and a new spirit. The New Testament picks this up and gives us fuller teaching on regeneration through God's Spirit, and the eternal life that is ours in Christ. So yes, there is hope for us through the life-giving Spirit of Christ.

The New Testament focuses mainly on the hope for *human beings* that comes through the work of Christ and the Holy Spirit. But it does not overlook the role of the Spirit in the wider creation, which is so prominent in the Old Testament, though of course the New Testament has more to say about Jesus Christ as the Word of God, as the agent and heir of creation. Let's conclude this chapter, however, by looking on to the role of the Spirit in the new creation. At this point we do need to turn to the New Testament, to its fuller vision of the future in the plan of God. But all that it says is built upon the foundation already laid in the Old Testament—including the teaching we have surveyed about the action of God's Spirit in creation. We turn to Romans 8:19-27, a key passage which links the Spirit and the new creation through the metaphor of labor pains and childbirth.

GROANING AND BIRTHING: THE SPIRIT AND NEW CREATION

> The creation waits in eager expectation for the sons of God to be revealed. For the creation was subjected to frustration, not by its own choice, but by the will of the one who subjected it, in hope that the creation itself will be liberated from its bondage to decay and brought into the glorious freedom of the children of God.
>
> We know that the whole creation has been groaning as in the pains of childbirth right up to the present time. Not only so, but we ourselves, who have the firstfruits of the Spirit, groan inwardly as we wait eagerly for our adoption as sons, the redemption of our bodies. . . .
>
> In the same way, the Spirit helps us in our weakness. We do not know what we ought to pray for, but the Spirit himself intercedes for us with groans that words cannot express. And he who searches our hearts knows the mind of the Spirit, because the Spirit intercedes for the saints in accordance with God's will. (Rom 8:19-23, 26-27)

This wonderful passage links together the resurrection of Christ with our own bodily resurrection and the redemption of the whole creation, and links them all with the Spirit. You might have thought that the word *joy* would be the dominant note in contemplating such a scenario. But the keyword in Paul's description is *groaning.* However, it is the groaning of labor pains, so the joy of birth lies ahead. These are the groans of gestation and birth. Yes, we live in this old world of sin and rebellion. But that old world is, in Paul's picture, the womb of the new creation, which is being brought to birth through Christ and the Spirit. And as Paul also says, if anyone is in Christ— new creation is already there (2 Cor 5:17)! We who are born again by God's Spirit through faith in Christ are part of the new creation that is being brought to birth.

There are actually three "groanings" in the passage:

1. Creation is groaning (Rom 8:22).

It is groaning, of course, because of our sin, as a result of which it has been subject to frustration in its prime purpose of giving glory to its Creator. And, as Hosea put it, even the land mourns and grieves because of the accumulated weight of human wickedness perpetrated on it and against it (Hos 4:1-3). But the groaning Paul is thinking of specifically is the groaning of childbirth. For the new creation is already gestating in the womb of the old. So the pain of creation *now* is in eager anticipation of the joy to come. Indeed, such pain is actually a guarantee of the joys ahead. For, as every mother and midwife knows, once labor pains have begun a birth is unstoppable.

2. We are groaning (Rom 8:23).

We too should groan because of our sin, but again Paul has a different groaning in mind. We groan in eager longing for that new creation which will mean the redemption of our bodies. It is so important in this passage to see that Paul does not talk about "the salvation of our souls," but the redemption of our bodies. Paul's expectation for the future is wholly creational. That is, he never sees salvation as a matter of *escaping out of* creation into some ethereal spiritual state. He rejected the kind of dualism that was prevalent in the Greek philosophical and religious culture of his day. No, God's redemption *embraces* his whole creation, and the resurrection of Jesus was the firstfruits of that great project. We human beings, therefore, will need new bodies to inhabit that new creation—and that is indeed what we look forward to. For, as he says elsewhere, we shall be transformed into the likeness of the risen Christ. His resurrection body is the prototype for the redemption of our bodies also (cf. Phil 3:21). This is why the Apostles' Creed so carefully says not, "I believe in the immortality of the soul" (which the ancient Greeks readily believed in) but "I believe in the resurrection of the body" (which they certainly did not).

3. The Spirit is groaning (Rom 8:26).

He is groaning within us as we live and pray—still living in the midst of this old creation with all its confusion and struggle, yet living also as the firstfruits, the advance guard of the new creation. For we too, if we are in Christ, are already participating in a reality that is still awaiting its full birthing in the future. For, as Paul also exclaims, "If anyone is in Christ, new creation!" (2 Cor 5:17, my translation).

So the whole metaphor is one of pain here and now but joy later. That is the essence of birth pains: hard labor followed by supreme joy as a new life bursts forth into the world. So the New Testament concept of our present suffering (which Paul has been talking about in Romans 8) is not just a matter of "stick it out here for a while, but soon you'll go to heaven when you die." Rather it is to recognize that God is bringing forth a whole new creation, redeemed by Christ and birthed by the Holy Spirit. And if we are in Christ and indwelt by the same Spirit, then we are already part of that new creation. And along with this wonderful old creation, we wait with impatient eagerness for that glorious birthday.

CONCLUSION

"Did you receive the Holy Spirit when you believed?" Paul asked the new believers at Ephesus (Acts 19:2). They had not even heard of him. We certainly have, so a more appropriate question for us might be, "Are you aware of what you have received when you received the Holy Spirit?" For we have now surveyed the scale and scope of what it is, or rather who it is, that you are asking to receive when you do.

The Holy Spirit, who lives in you if you are a child of God through faith in his Son Jesus Christ, is the Spirit of God who hovered over the very beginning of God's creation as it was spoken into existence. The universe itself owes its being to the Spirit of God.

The Holy Spirit is the one who has been constantly sustaining and renewing the creation ever since, so that the sun rose this morning for another new day and there was breakfast on your table.

The Holy Spirit is the one who gives life to every mortal creature that breathes on the planet, and who is the energy behind every breath you take in this life. And he is the one who gives life eternal to your mortal self, if you have put your faith in the crucified and risen Christ.

The Holy Spirit is the midwife of God's new creation, in which you will live in a resurrection body as part of God's new, redeemed humanity, and in which you will serve him and his creation as you were intended to.

This is the Holy Spirit, the Spirit of the God of the Bible. Do you know him?

2

The Empowering Spirit

Power. The word, like the thing itself, is much abused. Recently I heard a current affairs discussion on the radio in which someone said, "Power is the ability to make other people suffer." That is a rather cynical view, but it is probably quite close to popular feelings about people who wield "power." It implies that all power is evil and oppressive. But this is a false and dangerous misconception.

Power, basically, is neutral. It simply means the ability to do things. Power is needed if you are going to do anything good, as well as if it is used for evil. Power is the capacity to accomplish goals, or to influence the outcome of events and processes. That is why, when you find that you are unable do either of these things (accomplish your goals or influence events), you feel literally "power-less."

In one analysis of human motivation[1] (that is, theory about what motivates us to do what we do most of the time), power is one of three dominant motivations that, according to the theory, govern all we do. These are the things that get us up in the morning and make us feel that another day is worth living. These are the things that "make us tick." These are the things, conversely, that will leave us very frustrated if we cannot fulfill them over long periods of time. Each of us has a motivational profile in which these three prime mo-

---

[1]George New and David Cormack, *Why Did I Do That? Understanding and Mastering Your Motives* (London: Hodder & Stoughton, 1997).

tivators are differently configured. Some of us are almost entirely mo-
tivated by one, and very little by the other two; others of us have
more evenly distributed motivational drives. But in all of us, one of
these three is relatively predominant: (1) *achievement*—the desire to
get things done and accumulate a satisfying list of accomplished
goals; (2) *affiliation*—the desire for good relationships with others,
and enjoyment of company for its own sake, regardless of what gets
achieved; and (3) *power*—the desire to have an influence, make an
impact, change things in some way through our involvement.

Power, then, is effective action, making a difference, influencing
events, changing the way things are or will be. It is not surprising,
then, that the Spirit of God in the Old Testament is commonly linked
with power, for the biblical God is nothing if not effective in action
and in bringing about change! Indeed, when the Israelites spoke of
the Spirit of Yahweh, it was often simply a way of saying that God
himself was exercising his power on the earth, either directly or, more
commonly, through human agents. The Spirit of God is God's power
at work—either in direct action or in empowering people to do what
God wants to be done.

Empowering *people*. That's when the trouble starts. For human beings are not machines or robots. We are people to whom God has
given the very risky capacity for making up our own minds about
things and exercising our own choices. That was the power God gave
us when he created us, and sadly we abused it right up front. We took
power into our own hands by rebelling against God's authority, re-
jecting his instructions and choosing to decide for ourselves what we
will consider good and evil. The result of this tragic exercise of our
own power, which is usually called the Fall and is described in Genesis 3, is the terrible mess that we now live in. Every aspect of human
life (spiritual, physical, intellectual, emotional and social), has been

corrupted by sin. So all our boasted power is, spiritually speaking, our weakness—the weakness of sinful human nature.

And yet, it is human beings like us that God chooses to empower through his Spirit. The men and women in the Bible whom God empowered were just as much fallen sinners as you or I. With the single exception of Jesus Christ, to say that somebody was filled with, or empowered by, God's Spirit did not mean they were sinless, or that everything they subsequently did was morally perfect or precisely what God wanted in every respect. For when God's power and human weakness were combined in a single sinful human being, the results were not always predictable and were sometimes downright ambiguous. The reason is that the person in question, even when empowered by the Spirit of God, was still a fallen, sinful human being like you or me. If that was true in the Bible, how much more is it still true today? We shall need to come back to this point.

Let us then look first at some examples of people in whom the Spirit of God generated power and ability. Then we shall focus on the example of Moses in whom the Spirit of God produced a wonderful combination of power and humility.

POWER AND ABILITY

When some people in the Old Testament were said to have the Spirit of God, it simply meant that they had a God-given ability or competence or strength to do certain things for God or for his people. God's Spirit empowered and enabled them to do what had to be done.

Bezalel and Oholiab. Now it's very possible that you have never heard of the two gentlemen named Bezalel and Oholiab. But if you are interested in the Holy Spirit, you should have. For these are the first people in the Bible who are described as "filled with the Spirit of God." Being filled with the Spirit is something many Christians aspire to, though not many Christians expect the experience to do for them what it did for Bezalel and Oholiab. What did the filling of God's Spirit do in their lives? It enabled them to be craftsmen, working in metal and wood and precious stones, and all kinds of artistic design—and to be able to teach others the same skills. Here's the account:

> Then Moses said to the Israelites, "See, the LORD has chosen Bezalel son of Uri, the son of Hur, of the tribe of Judah, and *he has filled him with the Spirit of God,* with skill, ability and knowledge in all kinds of crafts—to make artistic designs for work in gold, silver and bronze, to cut and set stones, to work in wood and to engage in all kinds of artistic craftsmanship. And he has given both him and Oholiab son of Ahisamach, of the tribe of Dan, the ability to teach others. He has filled them with skill to do all kinds of work as craftsmen, designers, embroiderers in blue, purple and scarlet yarn and fine linen, and weavers—all of them master craftsmen and designers. So Bezalel, Oholiab and every skilled person to whom the LORD has given skill and ability to know how to carry out all the work of constructing the sanctuary are to do the work just as the LORD has commanded." (Ex 35:30—36:1, my italics)

Putting these things together like this gives great dignity to such skills. I love the fact that on this first occasion when the Spirit of God, which had been so active in all the wonderful craftsmanship of creation itself, is said to fill a human being, it is to enable that person to exercise the same kinds of delegated skills. There is something so wonderfully creative (and therefore God-like) in what this passage describes: craftsmanship, artistic design, embroidery with rich colors, carving wood and stone. I fondly wish I had some of these skills and greatly admire the work of artists who do. We should take seriously that these things are said to be marks of the filling of God's Spirit. Of course, Bezalel and Oholiab were so filled for the purpose of working on the tabernacle—the holy tent of God's presence among his people. But I don't think we need to limit the action of God's Spirit in this gifting only to "sacred" purposes. Presumably Bezalel and Oholiab had and exercised these skills before and after they were employed in constructing the tabernacle. The creation narrative, as we saw in the last chapter, portrays God himself as the universal master craftsman who rejoices in the goodness and beauty of all he has so wonderfully designed and executed. This text encourages us to believe that the same Spirit of God who was at work in creation is also at work in that same wider sense, in all those who, as human beings made in God's image, enrich our world with all kinds of creativity in art, music, colorful design, beautiful craftsmanship and—adding this to console myself in at least one area of creative endeavor—skillful speech and writing. When we honor and admire such art, we give glory to the Spirit who empowers it.

The judges. The judges were the men and women who were leaders among the tribes of Israel before they established a monarchy. They got a book named after them in the Old Testament. The word *judges* is not very helpful since it suggests stern patriarchs sitting behind large benches in stuffy courtrooms dealing with successions of criminals. In Hebrew the title meant simply someone who puts things right, by whatever means. This might include acting in a judicial or legal way to sort out disputes between people, or giving judgments on difficult local problems. But it could also include leading the people in battle against oppressive enemies, or calling the people to united action against some sudden threat. Some of them seem to have been fairly local heroes, whereas others rose to more national prominence and leadership.

One thing that is said quite often about these "judges" is that the Spirit of the LORD (Yahweh) would come upon them. When this happened it was a signal for action. Empowered by the Spirit of the LORD, they could exercise charismatic leadership and do valiant exploits that were recited around the campfires of Israel for generations to come. Here are some examples, all from the book of Judges:

> The Spirit of the LORD came upon [Othniel], so that he became Israel's judge and went to war. (Judg 3:10)

> Then the Spirit of the LORD came upon Gideon [literally it says, "clothed himself with Gideon"—God's Spirit put Gideon on like a coat!], and he blew a trumpet, summoning the Abiezrites to follow him. (Judg 6:34)

> Then the Spirit of the LORD came upon Jephthah. . . . He advanced against the Ammonites. (Judg 11:29)

> [Samson] grew and the LORD blessed him, and the Spirit of the LORD began to stir him while he was in Mahaneh Dan. (Judg 13:24-25)

> The Spirit of the LORD came upon [Samson] in power so that he tore the lion apart with his bare hands as he might have torn a young goat. (Judg 14:6)

> Then the Spirit of the LORD came upon [Samson] in power. He went down to Ashkelon, struck down thirty of their men, stripped them of their belongings and gave their clothes to those who had explained the riddle. Burning with anger, he went [home]. (Judg 14:19)

> The Spirit of the LORD came upon [Samson] in power. The ropes

on his arms became like charred flax, and the bindings dropped
from his hands. Finding a fresh jawbone of a donkey, he grabbed
it and struck down a thousand men. (Judg 15:14-15)

It is very clear that the Spirit of God is synonymous with power.
People do great things when the Spirit of Yahweh comes upon them.
But with Samson, something is very disturbing. In his case, power
means enormous physical strength. It starts innocently enough under the sign of God's blessing. But as the story proceeds, that strength
gets more and more out of control. Samson's human weakness is all
too visible under his superhuman strength.

In Uganda there is an advertisement for Pirelli tires that appears
on many large billboards along some roads. On the advertisement
there is a huge black fist with the knuckles pointing downward,
looking as if it's coming out of the picture at you. The base of each
knuckle takes the form of a massive tire with patterned tread, such
as you see on giant trucks. Beneath the image is the message
"Power is nothing without control." It has a point—spiritually too.
It's no good having superhuman powers if you lose control, lose
the plot and in the end lose the whole point of having the power
in the first place.

So here with Samson it seems that even Spirit-given power, power
that had been promised and given by God, can be misused and exploited for very questionable behavior. I don't think the narrator of
these stories means us to assume that God necessarily approved of all
that was done in the power of his Spirit. There is a growing excess in
Samson's raging violence. Not every manifestation of spiritual power
is unambiguously holy or wholesome. We will come back to that
point too.

Saul. Saul was the first king in Israel, but in many ways he was also the last of the line of judges. In his early days, he acted very much like the previous judges, and there is a kind of overlap between that era and the full-blown monarchy that really got going with David. So, just like the other judges, we read that "When Saul heard their words [about the threats of the Ammonites], the Spirit of God came upon him in power, and he burned with anger" (1 Sam 11:6). He then went out to win a great victory, as a result of which he was confirmed as king.

The initial role of the Spirit in the story of Saul is to authenticate Samuel's anointing him as king and to authorize his leadership. So we read,

> Then Samuel took a flask of oil and poured it on Saul's head and kissed him, saying, "Has not the LORD anointed you leader over his inheritance?" (1 Sam 10:1)

This is followed by a number of predicted signs that will confirm to Saul what Samuel has said and done, including:

> The Spirit of the LORD will come upon you in power, and you will prophesy with them, and you will be changed into a different person. (1 Sam 10:6)

Sure enough,

> As Saul turned to leave Samuel, God changed Saul's heart, and all these signs were fulfilled that day. When they arrived at Gibeah, a procession of prophets met him; the Spirit of God came upon him in power, and he joined in their prophesying.[2] (1 Sam 10:9-10)

---

[2]"Prophesying" at this early stage in Israel's life seems to have been a charismatic outpouring in a state of trance. Later it involved Saul stripping and lying prostrate on the ground with such prophets (1 Sam 19:19-24). It was not yet the clear and articulate delivery of a specific message from God that characterized later prophets.

But this initial authorization was later withdrawn by God in the wake of Saul's increasing disobedience and folly. So we are told that "the Spirit of the LORD had departed from Saul" (1 Sam 16:14) and in its place a very different kind of spirit afflicted Saul with God's permission—a spirit that took the form of dark moods, depression and murderous jealousy, and could also be linked to the strange phenomenon of "prophesying" (1 Sam 18:10-11).

So then, surveying this material, there is something mysterious about the manifestations of the Spirit of God at this earlier period of Israel's life. The Spirit of God, it seems, can be very good, positive and enriching, giving people ability, competence and power, or filling people for skillful and creative tasks. The Spirit can give people great powers of leadership and courage. The Spirit can also be unpredictable, sudden and surprising. The Spirit can be abused by those who run wild and willful, indulging in excess, out of control. And the Spirit can be withdrawn from those who persist in disobedience or folly.

There is something of a caution here for us. The power of the Spirit of God can be tied up with the very ambiguous powers of men. Not all so-called manifestations of the Spirit are in and of themselves welcome signs of the wholesome activity of God. They can be mixed up with the unwelcome manifestations of self-serving human ambition. And sometimes they can be deployed in ways that are out of control and potentially devastating.

We need wisdom and discernment. "Test the spirits," says John, "to see whether they are from God" (1 Jn 4:1). Not everyone, says Jesus, who claims to do miraculous wonders—often associated with the Spirit of God—is necessarily in the kingdom of God (Mt 7:21-23). We shall return to this warning again in the next chapter when we look more closely at the question of false prophets.

POWER WITH HUMILITY

The text for this section is really the whole story that we read in Numbers 11—14. It is a particular period in the turbulent life of Moses. You might find it helpful to pause and read through those chapters now. As you do so, you will notice the references to God's Spirit. There are not many, of course, and the narratives of Moses' life do not often refer to the Spirit of God. However, later Israelites were in no doubt at all that God had been very powerfully active through his Spirit in the life and work of Moses. Here, for example, is how a later prophet referred back to that era:

> Then his people recalled the days of old,
>> the days of Moses and his people—
> where is he who brought them through the sea,
>> with the shepherd of his flock?
> Where is he who set
>> his Holy Spirit among them,
> who sent his glorious arm of power
>> to be at Moses' right hand,
> who divided the waters before them,
>> to gain for himself everlasting renown,
> who led them through the depths?
> Like a horse in open country,
>> they did not stumble;
> like cattle that go down to the plain,
>> they were given rest by the Spirit of the LORD.
> This is how you guided your people
>> to make for yourself a glorious name. (Is 63:11-14)

The same passage, a little earlier, says that the people of Israel "rebelled and grieved his Holy Spirit" (Is 63:10). These are two of the very few occasions when the Spirit of God in the Old Testament is actually called his *Holy Spirit*. It is clear, of course, that the main focus of the Spirit's presence in this recollection is on the powerful acts of deliverance that Israel experienced—especially the exodus and the gift of the land. But it is equally important that the Spirit is linked to the role of Moses himself as the leader of Israel at that time. The power of God was exercised through the person of Moses. He was the human agent of God's Spirit. Moses, then, gives us a model of Spirit-filled leadership. He was clearly a leader of great power, given by God. And yet he served God faithfully—as Hebrews also testifies, "Moses was faithful as a servant in all God's house" (Heb 3:5).

What were some of the marks of the Spirit of God in the leadership of Moses that we can find in this section of narrative? Moses exercised great power, but, as we shall now see, it was power without personal pride, power without personal jealousy and power without personal ambition.

Power without pride.

Now Moses was a very humble man, more humble than anyone else on the face of the earth. (Num 12:3)

This is a remarkable testimonial. The word here translated "humble" is '*anaw*, and indeed it can mean meek and humble (e.g., in Prov 3:34 and Prov 16:19 where it is contrasted with "proud"). But most often it means, not so much a subjective virtue or an inward personal characteristic as an objective state inflicted by others. The word describes people who are lowly because of some affliction, people who suffer by being put down and demeaned by others (which was true enough of Moses a lot of the time, even as a leader):

> The vast bulk of the occurrences of this and related words de-
> note the position of people who have been humbled or afflicted
> in one way or another. It suggests people who are weak in some
> respect. They lack resources or power. . . . To say Moses was the
> lowliest person on earth [means that he] was just the most or-
> dinary of men, one of whom Yhwh made extraordinary de-
> mands, and on whom his people put extraordinary pressures.[3]

Is this not very ironic? Those who are lowly by definition "lack resources or power." Yet Moses was a man of incredible power. Even
secular historians would agree that Moses has to be included among
the greatest of all human leaders and nation builders. He was, after
Abraham, the "father of the nation"—the one who consolidated them
from a bunch of escaped slaves into a nation and led them to the
brink of their settlement in the land of Canaan. Moses was a leader,
and a very great one. Yet Moses was a servant, and a very lowly one.
A leader and a servant. A servant leader or a leading servant. Is it possible to be both? According to our text the answer is yes, because the
Bible affirms both of these paradoxical truths about him. The secret
of Moses' power lay in the Spirit of God, and the secret of his humility
lay in his lack of self-sufficiency.

Let's turn to our text. Numbers 11 describes just one more of the
many crises that Moses had to face. Like many human conflicts, it
revolved around our most basic human need—food. God had provided the people with manna. Their catering budget was a miracle
a day. But it was not enough. "The rabble with them began to crave
other food" (Num 11:4), as they remembered the menus of Egypt—

---

[3]John Goldingay, *Old Testament Theology, Volume One: Israel's Gospel* (Downers Grove, Ill.: Inter-
Varsity Press, 2003), p. 311.

fish, cucumbers, melons, leeks, onions and garlic (a healthy diet indeed, even if they were being whipped as slaves in the meantime). So they complained that they had lost their appetite and demanded meat. Moses, as usual, becomes the focus of their discontent. Here is the next challenge to his leadership, the next demand on his competence. What emergency plan can he come up with to solve this problem? Here is how the record describes his response. It is not flattering.

> Moses heard the people of every family wailing, each at the entrance to his tent. The LORD became exceedingly angry, and Moses was troubled. He asked the LORD, "Why have you brought this trouble on your servant? What have I done to displease you that you put the burden of all these people on me? Did I conceive all these people? Did I give them birth? Why do you tell me to carry them in my arms, as a nurse carries an infant, to the land you promised on oath to their forefathers? Where can I get meat for all these people? They keep wailing to me, 'Give us meat to eat!' I cannot carry all these people by myself; the burden is too heavy for me. If this is how you are going to treat me, put me to death right now—if I have found favor in your eyes—and do not let me face my own ruin." (Num 11:10-15)

What a litany of accusing questions! What a sarcastic ending ("if you love me, kill me now")! This is not "alpha male" leadership. This is not the calm assurance of a man who always knows exactly what he's going to do next, like James Bond. This is the panic of a man who has no clue where sufficient resources for the problem can be found. Self-sufficiency? Not an ounce.

Now this had not always been true of Moses. Think of him in his prime as the young prince of Egypt. Presented with a situation of obvious injustice, he knew exactly what to do. Summary justice. Instant execution of the offender. Two verses are all it takes to describe the whole incident: one for the problem, one for the solution (Ex 2:11-12). Problem spotted. Problem buried. Except that it wasn't, and Moses learned the hard way that quick reliance on his own solutions could result in long-term evacuation from any connection with the problem at all.

Meet Moses again, however, with his shoes off at the burning bush and he is different man, much chastened by forty years with his father-in-law's sheep and daughters. This time his sense of inadequacy is desperate and embarrassing. "Anyone but me, Lord," is the gist of his answer when God tells him it is time to return to Egypt and put *God's* solution into action.

Meet him on many occasions later when there is a problem. Where will you find him? Not setting up a committee to draft strategic plans and emergency rapid response tactics. Often you will find him flat on his face. So often we read the words, "Moses fell on his face before the LORD" (Num 14:5; 16:4, 22; 20:6). That is not the posture of the self-sufficient, though it suits the lowliest man on earth very nicely. Moses was a free man, and his greatest freedom was freedom from pride and self-sufficiency.

It was not because Moses had no gifts, no abilities of his own. We are not told anything explicitly about his upbringing at the court of Pharaoh by the Old Testament narrative, but Stephen draws the very probable inference that "Moses was educated in all the wisdom of the Egyptians and was powerful in speech and action" (Acts 7:22). Hebrews also imagines the life of Moses in the court of Pharaoh and talks about pleasures and treasures (Heb 11:25-26). So this was a man who probably spoke and wrote several languages, may well have been involved in international diplomacy and treaties, and had almost certainly been trained in the political and military arts of government. Not to mention the sheer physical vigor of the man that he was able to confront the might of an empire at the age of 80, and climb a mountain to scan the whole horizon with undimmed eyesight at 120. No doubt about it, Moses was a man of remarkable natural resilience.

But whatever his gifts and strengths, he did not depend on them. He found no reassurance in his own resources. Rather, he turned to God. And that was the best thing to do, for as the narrative tells us, God had the next step already worked out.

> The LORD said to Moses: "Bring me seventy of Israel's elders who are known to you as leaders and officials among the people. Have them come to the Tent of Meeting, that they may stand there with you. I will come down and speak with you there, and I will take of the Spirit that is on you and put the Spirit on them. They will help you carry the burden of the people so that you will not have to carry it alone." (Num 11:16-17)

This gives us two insights into Moses' humility:

1. *Dependence on God's Spirit.* We might not have known it from the earlier part of the story in this chapter, but the Spirit of God was "on Moses." Even Moses seems to have forgotten this. Perhaps it's easy to overlook your spiritual gifts when several hundred thousand people are demanding that you serve them up hot dinners (nonvegetarian, please). But this was indeed the answer, and the only one. Whatever might or might not happen next, only the power of God's Spirit could achieve it, for it was beyond the power of Moses to make anything happen at all.

But that is exactly the lesson that we learn here. Personal powerlessness is precisely the opportunity for God's power. Paul had learned this lesson very thoroughly also in his own battered career as a missionary.

> Such confidence as this is ours through Christ before God. Not that we are competent in ourselves to claim anything for ourselves, but our competence [or sufficiency] comes from God. . . . We have this treasure in jars of clay to show that this all-surpassing power is from God and not from us. (2 Cor 3:4-5; 4:7)
>
> He said to me, "My grace is sufficient for you, for my power is made perfect in weakness." Therefore I will boast all the more gladly about my weaknesses, so that Christ's power may rest on me. That is why, for Christ's sake, I delight in weaknesses, in insults, in hardships, in persecutions, in difficulties. For when I am weak, then I am strong. (2 Cor 12:9-10)

This idea has been well expressed in our own time through the words of a familiar worship song:

> He turns our weaknesses into his opportunities,
> so that the glory goes to him.[4]

2. *Acceptance of God's Spirit in others.* Moses needed to be willing at this point, not only to depend on God for himself personally, but also to depend on the help of others, to whom God would give a share of the same Spirit that Moses had. Spirit-filled leadership becomes shared leadership. Actually, this takes more humility than dependence on God alone. Some of us are very willing to trust *God.* Trusting *others,* who (we are asked to believe) also have the Spirit of God, feels like a much more dubious proposal. But it is one of the marks

---

[4]Graham Kendrick, "Rejoice," Kingsway's Thankyou Music, 1983.

of the Holy Spirit in anyone who is a servant-leader like Moses that they are humble enough to recognize God's gifts in others, and share leadership with them. *Pride* says, "If it can't be me and my power, then at least let it be my exclusive franchise of God's power. If I can't do it on my own, then let God do it, but make sure it's through me and nobody else." *Humility* says, "If God knows as well as I do that I can't do this alone, then let God provide Spirit-filled helpers for me— the more the better. I need them as much as I need God."

Power without jealousy. The story proceeds from one problem to another.

> So Moses went out and told the people what the LORD had said. He brought together seventy of their elders and had them stand around the Tent. Then the LORD came down in the cloud and spoke with him, and he took of the Spirit that was on him and put the Spirit on the seventy elders. When the Spirit rested on them, they prophesied, but they did not do so again.
>
> However, two men, whose names were Eldad and Medad, had remained in the camp. They were listed among the elders, but did not go out to the Tent. Yet the Spirit also rested on them, and they prophesied in the camp. A young man ran and told Moses, "Eldad and Medad are prophesying in the camp."
>
> Joshua, son of Nun, who had been Moses' aide since youth, spoke up and said, "Moses, my lord, stop them!" (Num 11:24-28)

Delegated leadership is all very well in theory. In practice it may lead to apparent chaos. Or at least to what are euphemistically called "circumstances beyond our control." Moses was willing to share the source of his leadership, the Spirit of God, and therefore also the practical outworking of his leadership. And that in itself, as we have just said, is a mark of his servant spirit and mature humility.

But then there is a sudden outburst of unscripted charismatic activity! It's a bit unclear exactly what was happening and why it was a problem. But if Moses and the other sixty-eight elders received the Spirit at the Tent of Meeting, which was outside the regular camp, then whatever Eldad and Medad were up to was beyond Moses' immediate observation or control. Things could easily get out of hand here. All this Spirit sharing is fine, provided it's kept under strict surveillance, right here where we can keep an eye on what's going on. But unauthorized, unsupervised, unofficial outbursts right in the midst of all the people in the camp could lead to, well, who knows where it might lead? And, perhaps with such thoughts, the voice of loud objection is raised by the number-two leader, Joshua: "Moses, my lord, stop them!"

What lies behind Joshua's rude interruption and urgent advice to Moses? We are not told, of course, but the narrator may be giving us a small clue in his reminder that Joshua had been Moses' assistant more or less all his life. Joshua's identity and status were entirely wrapped up with Moses. So perhaps he felt that his (Joshua's) own standing and authority were being threatened, if others were now going to be allowed to do what only Moses should do. Why, even he, Joshua (as far as we know), had not been privileged with such manifestations of the Spirit. So it was hardly fair that these outer ranks of leadership should suddenly enjoy them—especially if they hadn't even bothered to turn up in person! It is an interesting and common phenomenon that "big people" are often surrounded by their acolytes and groupies (whether deliberately or not). These latter—the special assistants, the minders and fixers—have a vested interest in keeping the big leader firmly on his pedestal. Anything that might diminish or dilute the authority of the number one is felt as an even bigger threat to the number two. So Joshua tells Moses to stop this danger-ous development, right now, with respect, sir.

Moses' reply is a classic:

> Are you jealous for my sake? I wish that all the LORD's people were prophets and that the LORD would put his Spirit on them! (Num 11:29)

I can't help thinking that there was a twinkle in Moses' eye as he put Joshua in his place. "Is it me you're really concerned about, or yourself? What is happening here is no problem for me; why is it a problem for you?" Moses had no personal jealousy, for his status, of-fice or privilege—or even for a monopoly of God's Spirit and his gifts. If God wanted others to enjoy (if that's the right word) the experience of his Spirit and all the manifestations that went with it, that's fine by Moses. They'll find out soon enough that it isn't all standing about prophesying, by any means. There is a lot of work to be done, not to mention all the hungry people out there. For the moment, whatever power God's Spirit would give Moses was power without jealousy. He would gladly share it. In fact, if God wanted to share the Spirit more widely still, he would welcome that too.

Again, I ponder what lay behind Moses' wish here. What led Moses to wish that God would democratize his Spirit in a strange an-ticipation of those later prophets who said God planned to do exactly that (as we shall see in chapter 5 below) and of the day of Pentecost when it actually happened?

Possibly it is evidence of Moses' reluctance to be a leader at all. This was not a job he had asked for, and he had done his best to de-cline it when it was first proposed. Was that an underlying attitude that never really left him? Yes, he was faithfully obeying God's call and leading this people, with the power of God's Spirit. But not because it was something he enjoyed or because he secretly relished being the "top guy." On the contrary, he would far rather have slipped back into the ranks and let others take over the leadership. So is his wish here a rather tongue-in-cheek comment that being the one with the Spirit of the LORD is not all it's made out to be? If everybody had the Spirit, maybe his own life would not be so unbearable as the butt of everybody else's problems. They could do their own prophesying and sort out their own mess. Even if this is all it means, it is a worthwhile point to ponder. The best leaders are often the most reluctant leaders, while those who hanker after all the power and status of leadership are usually the worst.

More likely, and more deeply, I think Moses' reply to Joshua is evidence of Moses' own profound security in his personal relationship with God. He had no personal jealousy as regards the Spirit of God, because he had no need to. Nothing could threaten or diminish what he and God shared in the intimacy of their relationship. God himself comments on this in the next chapter. He speaks warmly of Moses as

my servant Moses;
    he is faithful in all my house.
With him I speak face to face,
    clearly and not in riddles;
    he sees the form of the LORD. (Num 12:7-8)

Whatever the last mysterious line means, it undoubtedly speaks of a very close personal relationship between Moses and God. Moses knew who he was in himself, and he knew whose servant he was. In fact that *was* his identity—servant of the LORD. That was his status. Nothing could threaten or diminish that. He was utterly secure in that knowledge. Even when he was angrily protesting to God and ruefully suggesting that shooting him would be the most merciful option, he was living out the intimacy of that relationship. Only the closest friend of God would speak to him like that, eyeball-to-eyeball indeed (as the expression "face to face" literally reads in Hebrew). And Moses will do it again in Numbers 14 as we shall see.

So, with such deep and unshakable security in his relationship with God, Moses had no need for jealousy of others. He had no need to stand on his own authority or status or prerogatives. He had no need to monopolize the Spirit of God or the power it conferred. He could wield power *with humility* because he held power *without jealousy.*

There is a well-known paradox that bossiness is often a sign of insecurity. Those who are not secure in their own identity and relationships compensate for the inner inadequacy with excessive outer authoritarianism. Power-hungry control freaks deform human communities at all levels, sadly including Christian ones. Underneath the façade is often the attempt to prove something to themselves, the world, the church or God. "This is who I am because this is what I can do," or "This is how great I am because this is what I can make you do."

True humility, by contrast, is the sign of a person at ease with him- or herself and God. When you know that your own life is securely bound up with Christ in God and that nothing and nobody can rob you of it; when you know that your identity and security lie in God's grace, not in anything you can do to prove or earn either of them; when you can rest in the assurance that all things in heaven and earth are yours, and you are Christ's and Christ is God's (1 Cor 3:21-23); when these things fill your conscious and subconscious mind, what is there to be proud of? Who is there to be jealous of? What is there to be threatened by? What is there to worry about losing, when you cannot lose all this?

It has always seemed to me that the best way to learn humility is not to try. The paradox is that genuine, unselfconscious humility is the fruit of exalting and glorying in the status we have in Christ as children and servants of God. The more you revel in that status before God, the less you are bothered about preserving petty status before others. This is exactly the lesson that Jesus modeled and taught in washing his disciples' feet (Jn 13:3-15). John very carefully says that "Jesus knew that the Father had put all things under his power, and that he had come from God and was returning to God" (Jn 13:3). And the logic of his sentence is very clear. John does not say that *in spite of* knowing this, *nevertheless* Jesus washed their feet, but rather that *because* he knew these things he did so. It was because Jesus was so utterly secure in his relationship with his Father, so fully aware of his identity and his destiny, that he was the only person in the room who was inwardly free enough to do the work of a slave. The disciples were arguing jealously about who was the greatest. But because Jesus knew himself to be the Son of God, he was free to be the servant of men. That is power without jealousy, power to be the servant of others.

You want to be humble like Moses? You want to have the power that comes from God's Spirit, but to exercise it without pride and jealousy? Then fill your mind often with the knowledge that the Holy Spirit has made you a child of the living God. You are a son or daughter of the King of the universe. What more status do you need? Glory in that and humility will bloom quietly, unconsciously and fragrantly as the fruit of the same Spirit.

Power without ambition. The story moves forward yet again. The people reach the borders of the promised land. Spies are sent out in Numbers 13. But the majority report is filled with such alarm that the people refuse to go any further. So in Numbers 14 we find the people of Israel giving vent again to their endemic grumbling against Moses. At first they propose to choose another leader and return to Egypt. But when Moses and Aaron, along with Joshua and Caleb, try to persuade them not to rebel against the LORD and to go forward into the land, things get decidedly more ugly.

> The whole assembly talked about stoning them. Then the glory of the LORD appeared at the Tent of Meeting to all the Israelites. The LORD said to Moses, "How long will these people treat me with contempt? How long will they refuse to believe in me, in spite of all the miraculous signs I have performed among them? I will strike them down with a plague and destroy them, but I will make you into a nation greater and stronger than they." (Num 14:10-12)

Not for the first time, God proposed destroying these people and starting all over again with Moses. In Exodus 32—34, on the occasion of Israel's horrendous apostasy with the golden calf, right at the foot of Mount Sinai while Moses was up there getting the ten commandments, the same thing had happened. God in anger suggested getting rid of this nation of rebels and making a fresh start with Moses himself. These terrible occasions—at Sinai and here at Kadesh Barnea—burned themselves into Moses' memory. He recalls them both and the desperate intercessory response he had to make in Deuteronomy 9 when he reminds Israel, on the verge of going in to conquer the nations of Canaan, that if anybody deserved to be wiped out, it was they. It is worth reading Deuteronomy 9 to feel the passion of Moses' memories and the amazing grace of God's continued patience with this people.

It was an incredible temptation, if we can look at it like that. What was God proposing? He was offering to transfer to Moses the promise that he had made to Abraham (that he would be a great nation) and its implications. God still had his ultimate purpose in mind. But he would carry it out by a different route. Forget the tribes of Israel. From now on, it will be the children of Moses. He will be known as the God of Moses. Moses will be the patriarch of a new nation, his own descendants. Just God and Moses and his seed forever. And wouldn't they get on so well together, if only *these* people were finally out of the way? Such thoughts could easily have fed Moses' ambitions—if he'd had any. He could step away from the burdens of leadership of this rancorous mob, and step into the limelight of history.

How did Moses respond to God's combination of threat and offer? Numbers 14:13-19 gives his immediate answer. But the remembered version in Deuteronomy 9 is more structured, and ties it in with his similar prayer at Sinai, from Exodus 32. It shows how Moses answered God on both occasions.

> I lay prostrate before the LORD those forty days and forty nights because the LORD had said he would destroy you. I prayed to the LORD and said, "O Sovereign LORD, do not destroy your people, your own inheritance that you redeemed by your great power and brought out of Egypt with a might hand. Remember your servants Abraham, Isaac and Jacob. Overlook the stubbornness of this people, their wickedness and their sin. Otherwise, the country from which you brought us will say, 'Because the LORD was not able to take them into the land he had promised them, and because he hated them, he brought them out to put them to death in the desert.' But they are your people, your inheritance that you brought out by your great power and your outstretched arm." (Deut 9:25-29)

Moses not only refused God's offer, he virtually rebukes God for even making it. God had spoken of destroying "these people" (Num 14:11). Moses reminds God of just who "these people" actually are. Actually, Moses does a lot of reminding—which is not to suggest that God was suffering an attack of amnesia, but rather that Moses is doing what all intercessory prayer does—it appeals to those things we know are of supreme importance to God himself. So Moses says, "Remember Abraham"—the one to whom you swore on oath to bless his descendants and through them bless the world. You can't go back on that promise without denying your own self as God. "Remember the Egyptians"—in other words, God had a reputation to think of. The exodus had happened in the glare of international awareness (cf. Ex 15:14-15). If Yahweh God now turns and destroys the very people he had rescued, how will that look to the rest of the world? They will think that Yahweh is either incompetent or malicious. Is that the kind of reputation God wants? And above all, "Remember that these are *your* people." This is the clinching argument, emphasized again in Moses' final appeal: *your people, your inheritance.* Destroy these people, cautions Moses, and you will destroy your own future, for this is what you yourself have called your own special personal possession (Ex 19:5-6).

Moses had been called by God to serve God by serving *these* people. And he was not going to be deflected away from that calling—not even by God himself! He had no personal ambitions to be the father of a great nation in his own right. His job was to be the servant of God and the servant of *these* people—no matter what. But what people they were! Moses probably had the most critical, rebellious, awkward, ungrateful, unreasonable congregation of grumpy old men that any leader or pastor could ever have. Think of some of the things he has had to cope with in these narratives in the book of Numbers alone:

- Administrative overload
- Catering problems
- Charismatic outbursts
- Family feuds and disapproval of his own marriage
- Refusal to follow the vision God had given through him
- Rejection of his authority to speak for God
- Attacks from outside the community
- Sexual immorality within the community

And God suggests, "Let's get rid of all of that and all of them, and you can be the head of a new community altogether." Tragically, apart from actually killing people, that seems to be what some leaders do—whether leaders of churches or mission organizations. In fact that's how some of them became leaders in the first place—by jumping out of a church or organization they didn't like or one that caused them too many problems and just starting up a new one, preferably named after themselves (with "international" or "incorporated" tacked on to add importance). Any such temptation, any such ambition, is precisely what Moses flatly refuses here. The power of his leadership, and certainly the power of his intercession at this precise moment, was that it was power without selfish ambition. So Moses says to God, in effect, "Not interested. These are your people. You called me to serve them and lead them, and that is what I will do. So please don't dangle alternative scenarios before me."

I am reminded of the example of Jesus, who also had to put up with a lot of grief from his followers. In the end, one of them betrayed him, one of them denied him, and all the rest ran away at the crucial moment. And yet Jesus remained utterly committed to them, so that in his final hours he could affirm to his Father that he had lost not one of them, except Judas, who had excluded himself (Jn 17:12). Or we might recall the similar example of the apostle Paul. It was to the Christians at Corinth, who had caused him endless problems (including some that involved misunderstanding and abuse of the gifts of the Spirit and some that were very similar to those faced by Moses) that Paul nevertheless wrote the astonishing words, "We [preach] . . . ourselves as your servants for Jesus' sake" (2 Cor 4:5). He was appalled at the thought that some of them even wanted to use his name as a slogan for their faction. "What, after all, is Apollos? And what is Paul? Only servants . . ." (1 Cor 3:5).

You may perhaps be in some form of Christian leadership. You are certainly in some form of ministry, for all disciples of Jesus are. This is a good point to do a motivational profile on yourself. What drives your work? What are your ambitions? To serve God and his people? That sounds great, but is it a concealed ego booster, or is it a total dedication to *these* people—the real, gritty, grainy people whom God has entrusted to you? Is your leadership a life of very particular servanthood to a very particular people—like Moses?

CONCLUSION

The paradox of the power of Moses, then, is this. The greatest evidence of the *presence* of the Holy Spirit in his life was precisely the *absence* of those things that are commonly linked with great and powerful people: pride in one's own self-sufficiency, jealous defense of one's own prerogatives, driving ambition for one's own legacy. This is the power of the Holy Spirit in a human life. This is power *with* humility.

The church needs leaders. And leaders need power, if they are ever to get anything done (or, more properly, if God is ever to get anything done through them). But the kind of power they need is not the kind of power by which the world generally assesses leadership—"Not by might nor by power, but by my Spirit," says the LORD (Zech 4:6).

Pray for those whom God has called into positions of leadership among his people, including yourself if appropriate, that there will be much greater evidence of the empowering Spirit of God, and much less evidence of the ambiguous and dangerous power of our fallen human weaknesses. May we be filled with the power of God's Spirit, in the likeness of Moses, and of Jesus.

3

The Prophetic Spirit

> Above all, you must understand that no prophecy of Scripture
> came about by the prophet's own interpretation. For prophecy
> never had its origin in the will of man, but men spoke from God
> as they were carried along by the Holy Spirit. (2 Pet 1:20-21)

Peter tells us here that the prophets of the Old Testament did not
make up their own messages out of their heads or imaginations.
Rather, he affirms the double authorship of the Scriptures: "*Men
spoke from God.*" It was human beings who did the speaking, but it
was God who provided the message. The words they spoke and
wrote were therefore their own freely chosen words, but those words
conveyed what God wanted to be said. And the means by which this
happened, Peter adds, was the power of the Holy Spirit, carrying
these prophetic speakers and writers along.

The New Testament, then, affirms the work of the Spirit of God in
the Old Testament, not only in creation (chapter 1), not only in
works of power and leadership (chapter 2), but also in the revelation
of God's word. Paul tells us that the Spirit searches the deep things of
God. For "no one knows the thoughts of God except the Spirit of
God" (1 Cor 2:10-11). God's Spirit, then, is the agent of communication from God's mind, with God's word, through God's prophets, to
God's people.

In the Old Testament the prophets were key transmitters of this communication. Of course, they were not the only ones through whom the Holy Spirit communicated God's revelation. God's Spirit was at work in those who wrote the narratives, those who framed the law, those who composed the psalms, those who gathered words of wisdom, and so on. All Scripture is breathed out by God through his Holy Spirit (2 Tim 3:16). However, the distinctive mark of the prophets is that they made the direct verbal claim, "Thus says the Lord"—meaning that the words which then followed from their mouth or pen constituted the direct message of God himself. So in this chapter we shall look at the work of the Spirit in the ministry of the prophets.

> As for me, I am filled with power,
>> with the Spirit of the LORD. (Mic 3:8)

Micah here makes exactly the claim that 2 Peter 1:21 refers to. He has been commissioned to speak to Israel, and he is filled with the Spirit of the LORD to do so. Remarkably, however, such a direct claim on the lips of a prophet is quite rare. The only other example is Isaiah 48:16, where the prophet says, "Now the Sovereign LORD has sent me, with his Spirit." Isaiah 61:1 is another possibility, but it is most likely that the prophet is there speaking with the voice of the coming Servant of God, rather than directly of himself (which is most likely the case in Isaiah 48:16). Why is this? Why is it that the prophets of the Old Testament, especially the early ones, hardly ever actually claim to be speaking by the Spirit of God, even though the New Testament affirms that they were? Why is this claim so rare?

One probable reason is the problem that all the genuine prophets of God faced, namely the presence of false prophets among the people. Micah, in the same context as his own claim, refers to them scathingly:

As for the prophets
　　who lead my people astray,
if one feeds them,
　　they proclaim "peace";
if he does not,
　　they prepare to wage war against him.
Therefore night will come over you, without visions,
　　and darkness, without divination.
The sun will set for the prophets,
　　and the day will go dark for them.
The seers will be ashamed
　　and the diviners disgraced.
They will all cover their faces
　　because there is no answer from God. (Mic 3:5-7)

These were people who claimed to speak from God, and very probably claimed the Spirit of God when doing so (e.g., 1 Kings 22:24), but who did not bring the true word of God at all—on the contrary, they undermined and perverted it. Possibly for this reason, most of the prophets whose words we now have in our Bible preferred to talk about "the word of the LORD" as an objective reality, rather than claim the more subjective experience of the Spirit of the LORD.

So then, in order to see this contrast clearly and therefore appreciate what the true prophetic Spirit was like, we need to look first of all at the phenomenon of false prophecy. It will be a rather grim task, but exposing falsehood is always a necessary part of exalting the truth. We shall find that the problem of false prophecy did not end with the Old Testament, and there are good lessons for us to learn here to help us be discerning in our own response to prophetic claims today.

FALSE PROPHETS AND THEIR OWN SPIRIT

"Woe to the foolish prophets who follow *their own spirit* and have seen nothing!" declares God through Ezekiel (Ezek 13:3, my italics). There are many texts denouncing false prophets. You may find it helpful (though probably depressing) to read through the following primary passages before we come to a thematic analysis of what they (and others) have to say about the false prophets in Israel: Jeremiah 23:9-32, Ezekiel 13 and Micah 2:6-11.

We can identify three major features that marked out these prophets as false, as not having come from God, as dangerously misleading to the people. All of them are worth reflecting on today.

Lack of personal moral integrity. The lives of these people who claimed so much were actually sensual and ill-disciplined. By the standards of God's law they were not even good Israelites, let alone good prophets. For example, they were guilty of:

- *Drunkenness.* The only spirit they knew was the trio of wines, beers and spirits.

  Priests and prophets stagger from beer
      and are befuddled with wine;
   they reel from beer,
      they stagger when seeing visions,
      they stumble when rendering decisions.
  All the tables are covered with vomit
      and there is not a spot without filth. (Is 28:7-8; cf. Mic 2:11)

- *Sexual immorality.* They made public pronouncements, but lived in private sin.

  Among the prophets of Jerusalem
      I have seen something horrible:
      They commit adultery and live a lie. (Jer 23:14)

- *Greed.* They were prepared to sell their clever words to the highest bidder. They claimed to have the word of God, and yet they had no shame in offering to "sell" it, like street-vendors or prostitutes.

Her leaders judge for a bribe,
>   her priests teach for a price,
>   and her prophets tell fortunes for money.
>   (Mic 3:11; cf. Jer 6:13)

So they lacked personal moral integrity. How then could they dare to speak on behalf of the God of all truth and integrity? How could they live in immorality and yet presume to represent the Holy One of Israel? How could they live in grasping greed and have any contact with the heart of the God who cared for the poor and needy?

"By their fruit you will recognize them," said Jesus (Mt 7:16). We also need to be watchful and discerning regarding those who claim to have, or are paraded as having, great "prophetic ministries." We are right to inquire whether there is personal moral integrity along with the great public persona. We are right to be suspicious if there are hints of questionable behavior, the whiff of fraud or corruption, or evidence of a greedy, opulent lifestyle. The Holy Spirit is not at all honored by, or even present in, those who use his name to feed their own lusts or line their own pockets.

Now it is important not to say this simply as a blanket condemnation. I am not saying we should expose other people's false claims in order to point with smug relief to our own superiority. That is the Pharisees' attitude, and Jesus condemned such self-righteousness mercilessly. Nor am I claiming for a moment that only those who are morally perfect can engage in any Spirit-filled ministry. If that were the case, the ranks of those who could do so would be very thin indeed. In fact there would be no ranks at all, for all of us are sinners and all of us fall short of God's standards of personal integrity. I am a sinner saved by grace, as much as you are, or any other person in ministry. In fact, if being morally blameless were the criterion, none of the Bible would have been written, because it too was written by people who were sinners. The question is, however, are we repentant sinners? Are we forgiven sinners? Do we know what it is to have been on our face before the Lord, begging for his mercy and restoration? Are we seeking to walk in the light? Are we daily conscious of our sin, but daily striving to please our Lord? The test then, is whether there is a clear *determination* to walk in integrity, to live by the moral standards of God's word, to repent humbly and quickly when we fail, and to put things right in the sight of God and the church. That is what is lacking in these false prophets, ancient and modern. We need to know that the words that are claimed to be words from God are coming from the mouths of those who know their own unclean lips and unclean hearts and have had both cleansed by the grace of God. We need to know that whatever ministries people have or claim, they are being exercised by those who know themselves to be forgiven failures and who live with a sense of grateful astonishment that God should use them at all

Lack of public moral courage. These prophets caught the mood of the public at any given time and then simply reflected it, echoing it back to willing listeners who were only too pleased to have their opinions endorsed by apparent spokespeople for the Almighty. They never challenged or rebuked that public mood or that dominant social consensus, even when it was clearly in breach of the known laws and will of God.

During the era of the great Old Testament prophets, the nation of Israel (including both kingdoms—Israel in the north and Judah in the south) stood in great danger of God's imminent judgment. All kinds of social rottenness were devouring their society. There was economic oppression and exploitation of the poor. There was a succession of appalling governments that ranged from incompetent to vicious. There was blatant corruption of the judicial system by the wealthy. There was degrading sexual immorality under religious pretexts and the accompanying horror of child sacrifice. And underlying it all there was rampant spiritual apostasy as Israelites at every level broke faith with the LORD, their covenant God and Redeemer, to go after other gods and idols. The nation was an absolute mess and in very great danger.

But these alleged prophets, when asked to comment, were not at all alarmed. "It's OK," they chorused. "God is not bothered. All is well" (cf. Jer 5:12). It was as if their nation was bleeding to death from a gaping wound and all they could offer was a strip of sticking plaster.

> They dress the wound of my people
>   as though it were not serious.
> "Peace, peace," they say,
>   when there is no peace.
> Are they ashamed of their loathsome conduct?
>   No, they have no shame at all;
>   they do not even know how to blush. (Jer 6:14-15)

Far from offering any radical solution to the festering problems of their society, they themselves were part of the problem, for they acquiesced in its evil by condoning it.

> They keep saying to those who despise me,
>   "The LORD says: You will have peace."
> And to all who follow the stubbornness of their hearts
>   they say, "No harm will come to you." (Jer 23:17)

Ezekiel says that all the efforts of these prophets to reassure the people in spite of their wickedness were like building a wall that is so flimsy it is bound to collapse (the sin of the nation), and then just whitewashing over the cracks in the hope nobody will notice (the words of the prophets). A shower of rain will wash off the whitewash and reduce the whole thing to rubble. Then those who built it and those who whitewashed it will both be crushed in the devastation (Ezek 13:10-16).

We too live in a society that turns moral values upside down. Certainly that is true of contemporary Western society. It has become a society where basic human goodness is mocked and God's standards for family and community life are attacked and vilified. It is a society where all kinds of practice that is contrary to God's best will for human life and human relationship is advocated and encouraged. It is a society that manages to live in obscene wealth and luxury while fully conscious of the poverty and suffering of the majority of the human race. It is a society in bondage to massive public idolatries to the false gods of mammon (consumerism), military hopes for security and national pride.

And we too have religious figures who engage in the same double deception that false prophets inflicted on Israel: those who *discourage* the righteous with lies and threats and *encourage* the wicked in their ways while failing to warn them of the consequences. This is exactly what Ezekiel observed as so sickening to God, and as something that only God could rescue his people from.

> Because you *disheartened the righteous* with your lies, when I had brought them no grief, and because you *encouraged the wicked* not to turn from their evil ways and so save their lives, therefore . . . I will save my people from you hands. And then you will know that I am the LORD. (Ezek 13:22-23)

Lack of any prophetic mandate from God. There is a gaping credibility gap in relation to these prophets, between the claims and the truth, between the charade and the reality. They claim to have come from God, but God has never seen them in his presence. They announce that they speak in God's name, but God has never sent them. They wear the prophetic mantle, but they have no prophetic mandate.

> Which of them has stood in the council of the LORD
>> to see or to hear his word?
>> Who has listened and heard his word? . . .
>
> I did not send these prophets,
>> yet they have run with their message;
> I did not speak to them,
>> yet they have prophesied.
> But if they had stood in my council,
>> they would have proclaimed my words to my people
> and would have turned them from their evil ways
>> and from their evil deeds. (Jer 23:18, 21-22)

> Their visions are false and their divinations a lie. They say, "The LORD declares," when the LORD has not sent them; yet they expect their words to be fulfilled. Have you not seen false visions and uttered lying divinations when you say, "The LORD declares," though I have not spoken? (Ezek 13:6-7)

Here, then, are people who are not sent by God, and yet they have a great deal to say. They never stop talking. They have the public ear and dominate the national media. They are not short on content. But if God didn't send them, where does it all come from? Whatever spirit they claim is certainly not the Holy Spirit of God. If any spirit is involved, it is "their own spirit"—i.e., their own imaginings, their dreams, their weird and wonderful ideas. They sound most impressive, but there is no substance, only wind (Jer 5:13) and self-delusion. Worse, much of what they say is not even original, but swapped and stolen from one another. The only thing worse than nonsense is second-hand nonsense. Unlike recycled garbage that can at least be made productive, this re-cycling of so-called prophetic messages remains useless no matter how many times you hear it.

> "I have heard what the prophets say who prophesy lies in my name. They say, 'I had a dream! I had a dream!' How long will this continue in the hearts of these lying prophets, who prophesy the delusions of their own minds? . . . Let the prophet who has a dream tell his dream, but let the one who has my word speak it faithfully. For what has straw to do with grain? . . . I am against the prophets who steal from one another words supposedly from me. . . . I am against those who prophesy false dreams," declares the LORD. "They tell them and lead my people astray with their reckless lies, yet I did not send or appoint them. They do not benefit these people in the least," declares the LORD. (Jer 23:25-26, 28, 30, 32)

What a catalog. What an indictment. But this is religion without the Spirit of God. This is religion that endorses the social status quo without challenge, and leaves the people without the living word of God. This kind of so-called prophetic activity is not pleasing to God—he is against it. It is not owned by God—he neither called them nor sent them. Rather, those who indulge in it are called to repent or else be judged along with those they have so cruelly deceived.

These Old Testament warnings about false prophets are still very relevant today. We are assailed by falsehoods masquerading as some new revelation from God. I am not thinking only of speculative books and theories that reach incredible levels of popularity in the secular arena, such as *The Da Vinci Code*. Far more damaging are books, films, and websites from Christian sources that distort the Bible at a fundamental level and then build fantasy on that distortion to feed our fascination with the future. And they do this in spite of Jesus' warning not to waste time speculating about his return, but simply to be prepared for it by getting on with the job he entrusted to us. These books, backed up by all the power of consumerist merchandising, sell by the millions, like fast food, and make their authors and publishers millionaires. But they distract and mislead God's people into obsessions with so-called prophetic signs and end-time scenarios, while at the same time doing little to address the screaming suffering and injustices of our world, or the rampant evil in the very societies where such "prophetic" books and ministries proliferate.

Then there are the televangelists and purveyors of prosperity "gospel" (an abuse of the term, since it is far from good news), appealing to, and exploiting for profit, people's innate material greed in the name of God's blessing. Add to that the inflated claims and grossly insensitive publicity of some of the great "healing miracle" merchants. And even at the lowly level of ordinary local churches there are those who abuse the Holy Spirit by claiming his authority for their latest "revelation" or for the latest fashionable theory, style, song or method.

We should remember the sobering warning of Jesus that not all who claim his name are what they seem:

> Not everyone who says to me, "Lord, Lord," will enter the kingdom of heaven, but only he who does the will of my Father who is in heaven. Many will say to me on that day, "Lord, Lord, did

we not prophesy in your name, and in your name drive out demons and perform many miracles?" Then I will tell them plainly, "I never knew you. Away from me, you evildoers! (Mt 7:21-23)

I find this one of the most sobering, even frightening, parts of the Bible. Jesus says it is possible to have a great so-called prophetic ministry—ostensibly in the name of Christ—and yet not belong to the kingdom of God. Jesus says it is possible to have a great deliverance ministry and yet not be owned by Jesus. Jesus says it is possible to do great miracles and yet not be doing the will of our Father in heaven. Jesus says it is possible to claim to be doing ministry in his name and yet to be disowned and dismissed by him as an evildoer.

I doubt if I would have the courage to say such things in the face of so much that is claimed today as "mighty ministries." So I am glad Jesus said these words, not me. They are terribly scary words. Jesus says this will not be just a minor irritation, but a common problem: "*Many* will say to me. . . . And I will tell them, 'I never knew you.'" And if Jesus does not know them, then they certainly do not know him.

What does this call for? It means we simply must be discerning about all ministry claims and the alleged statistics that so often go along with them. We should ask, "Where is the fruit? Where are the changed lives? Where is the evidence of the work of the *Holy* Spirit? Where are the people who are now more like Jesus, more committed to the love, compassion, justice and integrity of God and God's kingdom?" And, of course, it means that we must also be ruthlessly honest with our own motives and ambitions in ministry. There is a rather old-fashioned saying that talks about someone being "mightily used by God for his glory." Well, it can be wonderfully true. But there are times when I look at some great and prominent people for whom this claim is made, and I wonder just who is being used by whom—and for whose glory.

GOD'S PROPHETS AND GOD'S SPIRIT

At last, and with some relief, we can turn from our doleful survey of false prophets and their own spirit, to the more cheerful side of our theme—the fact that there were true prophets of God who did indeed perform their ministry through the Holy Spirit of God. At the beginning of the last chapter we saw that later prophets looked back and saw the work of the Holy Spirit in the life and leadership of Moses (Is 63:10-14). In relation to the prophets themselves, it is interesting that although they hardly ever claimed the Spirit of God for themselves, it was recognized in the later Old Testament that it was indeed through God's Spirit that true prophets had spoken.

This is a point that Nehemiah makes in his great prayer of confession with reference to both Moses and the prophets. Speaking of the time of Moses and the years in the wilderness Nehemiah says, "You gave *your good Spirit* to instruct them" (Neh 9:20, my italics). The reference is undoubtedly to the role of Moses in teaching Israel the law. Nehemiah says he did it by God's "good Spirit"—which connects with what we saw in the last chapter about the Spirit on Moses in Numbers. Speaking of the later centuries of Israel's history, Nehemiah laments the fact that

> for many years you were patient with them. *By your Spirit* you admonished them through your prophets. Yet they paid no attention. (Neh 9:30, my italics)

Moses, of course, was himself a prophet—the first great prophet indeed in the long line that led eventually to Jesus. So in both verses

Nehemiah is describing prophetic ministry—as *teaching* (from Moses in Neh 9:20) and *warning* (from the prophets in Neh 9:30). And he sees both these tasks as essentially the work of God's Spirit. Here, then, we have the true source of the ministry and message of those who were true spokespersons for God. We have just seen some of the ugly marks of the *false* prophets who lacked God's Spirit. They lacked personal moral integrity, public moral courage and a prophetic mandate from God. What then were the marks of the *true* prophets who were filled with the Spirit? A long list might be drawn up of the finer points of Old Testament prophets, but I want to focus on texts where a connection is specifically made between prophets and the Spirit of God. And in that regard, I think two points are outstanding. Because they were speaking by the Spirit of the LORD God, true prophets had (1) a compulsion to speak the truth and (2) the courage to stand for justice.

Compulsion to speak the truth. Our example for this point may seem somewhat surprising. The person we have in mind was not even an Israelite. Yet in the story of his encounter with Israel from a safe distance, we are explicitly told that he was filled with the Spirit of God (Num 24:2)—the God of Israel. His name was Balaam, and he was a prophet of sorts—a seer or diviner who lived far to the east in Mesopotamia. You can read his whole story in Numbers 22—24.

When the Israelites camped in the plains of Moab on their way toward the land of Canaan, the local king of Moab, Balak, "was terrified because there were so many people" (Num 22:2-3). As it turned out, he need not have feared, since Israel had instructions not to conquer Moab but to pass through it on their journey (Deut 2:9). However, Balak in his fear turned to sorcery and hired Balaam to put a curse on Israel. Balaam's reputation in such matters was apparently gold standard (Num 22:6). Balak had obviously not heard of the boomerang danger of such a tactic, for God had promised Abraham that "whoever curses you I will curse" (Gen 12:3).

Balaam makes three attempts to curse Israel, while Balak promises to pay ever higher fees in ever increasing frustration. All three attempts are abortive since Balaam finds he can do nothing but bless Israel. In the end he gives up, forfeits his fee, delivers a few final oracles and sets off for home a wiser, and perhaps humbler, man.

The interesting point for our purpose here is that Balaam was instructed in advance to be careful to say only what God told him. And then, when he is filled with the Spirit of God, he finds that he cannot do anything else but speak the truth from God. His altercations with Balak make the point with some humor, as Balak gets angrier with every failed attempt to get what he had paid for.

> Balak said to Balaam, "What have you done to me? I brought you to curse my enemies, but you have done nothing but bless them!"
>
> He answered, "Must I not speak what the LORD puts in my mouth?" (Num 23:11-12)

> Then Balak said to Balaam, "Neither curse them at all nor bless them at all!"
>
> Balaam answered, "Did I not tell you I must do whatever the LORD says?" (Num 23:25-26)

> Then Balak's anger burned against Balaam. He struck his hands together and said to him, "I summoned you to curse my enemies, but you have blessed them these three times. Now leave at once and go home! I said I would reward you handsomely, but the LORD has kept you from being rewarded."

Balaam answered Balak, "Did I not tell the messengers you
sent me, 'Even if Balak gave me his palace filled with silver and
gold, I could not do anything of my own accord, good or bad,
to go beyond the command of the LORD—and I must say only
what the LORD says'?" (Num 24:10-13)

That is the mark of someone truly filled by the Spirit of God. Balaam, then, though a non-Israelite, can be seen here as a model for
every true Israelite prophet (and we could certainly wish that the lim-
its Balaam articulated for himself were true of every Christian
preacher as well). Micaiah said exactly the same thing when he was
hauled before Ahab and Jehoshaphat for a prebattle blessing (1 Kings
22:14). The irony in that story is that Ahab insisted on hearing the
truth and then deliberately (and fatally) chose to ignore it. But by ig-
noring it he brought about its fulfillment.

Also interesting is what Balaam says in his oracles, when the Spirit
of God came upon him (Num 24:2):

How can I curse
    those whom God has not cursed?
How can I denounce
    those whom the LORD has not denounced? (Num 23:8)

God is not a man, that he should lie,
    nor a son of man, that he should change his mind.
Does he speak and then not act?
    Does he promise and not fulfill?
I have received a command to bless;
    he has blessed, and I cannot change it. (Num 23:19-20).

Balaam, speaking by the Spirit, cannot curse those whom God has
blessed. Sadly today we have religious leaders who feel free to bless

what God has condemned and claim the enlightenment of the Spirit in doing so.

So then, as early as the time of Israel in the wilderness we find a lesson in what happens when someone exercises prophetic gifts under the control of the Spirit of God. They have a compulsion to speak the truth—even if they come out of a pagan background.

A far greater body of truth, however, had already been communicated through that other, much greater, Spirit-filled prophet in these narratives—Moses himself. That is, the Torah—the law of God, given at Sinai. Paul calls the law "the embodiment of knowledge and truth" (Rom 2:20). No wonder, for Nehemiah says the law was taught by the Spirit (Neh 9:20), and he is the Spirit of truth.

This great legacy of God's law in the Old Testament—unprecedented and unparalleled (Deut 4:32-33; Ps 147:19-20)—underlies all the rest of the Old Testament. The law formed the foundation for the preaching of the prophets, provided the evaluating criteria for the history writers and watered the roots of Israel's worship. And all of this has been bound together within the Scriptures we now hold in our hands. The Scripture comes to us as the word of God, through the Spirit of God. And because those who spoke and wrote by the Spirit were under the compulsion of the truth of God himself, this word is truth. As truth, the word of God in the Scriptures is trustworthy and is given in order to form the foundation of all our thinking, believing and behaving. It is this word of truth that shapes our worldview as believers and thus governs how we see everything else in life. The Word of God is the platform on which we build the whole of our lives.

The truth and trustworthiness of God's word is one of the most precious things the writer of Psalm 119 celebrated in his great poem.

The statues you have laid down are righteous;
   they are fully trustworthy. . . .
Your righteousness is everlasting
   and your law is true. . . .
All your words are true;
   all your righteous laws are eternal. (Ps 119:138, 142, 160)

For this reason the psalmist confidently builds his whole life upon it. Jesus held the same belief as the psalmist about God's word. "Your word is truth," said Jesus to his Father (Jn 17:17), having already acknowledged the work of the Spirit of God in the delivery of truth (Jn 16:13).

Is that what you believe? That God's word, which we now have in Scripture, is true and trustworthy? It's what Jesus believed. It's what the psalmists, the prophets, Moses and even Balaam believed (not to mention his donkey). It is a fundamental part of the Christian faith that God has not left us in the darkness of ignorance or error. Rather, as Peter reminded us at the beginning of this chapter, God has spoken through human beings who were carried along by the Spirit as they spoke and wrote. And the essential mark of that Spirit-controlled utterance is truth and trustworthiness. But it is not enough just to give mental assent to it, merely by repeating after me, "I believe the Bible is true." At least two further steps need to be taken.

First of all, are you building your whole life, in all its dimensions, on the truth of the Word of God? Is your worldview shaped by the Bible? Is the Bible not merely the object, but the subject, of your thinking? That is to say, the Bible should be not only something we *think about*, but something we *think with*. It is to provide the foundations for how we think about everything else and is to be the guide to how we act in all circumstances.

Second, are you testing all the claims and teachings you encounter—in books, tapes or other media, from the pulpit or from celebrity Christian communicators—*by the truth of the Bible?* The best example to follow is that of the Bereans. When they had heard the apostle Paul preaching, sure, "they received the message with great eagerness." But even though it was from Paul, they still "examined the Scriptures every day to see if what Paul said was true" (Acts 17:11). For only the Scriptures would prove the truth or otherwise of his words—even the words of an apostle. Is that what you do? Scripture is the reality checkpoint to which you should invite all claims for your allegiance to accompany you. You read an intriguing Christian book with highly persuasive praise on its cover. Yes, but, you should be asking yourself, is that what the Bible really says? And if the book builds its case on a few Bible passages, is that what the Bible, taken as a whole in context, really means? Is it true to the whole message of Scripture or is it a distortion achieved by twisting one part of the Bible out of context and out of proportion?

I don't mean to turn us all into cynics who can *never* accept or believe anything. The problem is, it seems to me, that too many Christians are only too *quick* to accept and believe anything and everything. My plea is simply for a greater discernment, remembering the words of Jesus: not everything that claims his name is necessarily owned by him. Not everything that claims the Spirit comes from the Spirit of truth. Fortunately, the same Spirit of truth who spoke through the prophets and inspired the Scriptures also takes up residence in every believer. So it is one of the marks of the work of the Holy Spirit in our lives that he convinces us of the truth of his own word and leads us into truth. But he is not the Spirit of contradiction. That is why it is proper to weigh up all prophetic words that claim to be given by the Spirit and to test them against the Scriptures.

The courage to stand for justice. God sent his prophets to expose the wickedness of his people and to warn them of its dire consequences. Such a task was unpopular and costly. Far easier to be one of the cheerful prophets of peace and prosperity. Nobody likes to be exposed or challenged. And nobody likes to be the whistle-blower when others are doing wrong. And yet, under that Spirit-filled compulsion to speak the truth, the prophets had to do it and did it with courage. Of the prophets who lived before the exile, Amos suffered ecclesiastical anger and deportation; Hosea suffered intense marital pain as the cost of the message his broken marriage symbolized; Jeremiah suffered family hostility and death threats, political ostracism, physical abuse and life-threatening incarceration; one of Jeremiah's contemporaries, Uriah, was put to death for the same message (Jer 26:20-23).

Looking back on that era of prophecy before the exile, Zechariah sums up both the message they brought and the rejection they experienced:

> "'Are these not the words the LORD proclaimed through the earlier prophets when Jerusalem and its surrounding towns were at rest and prosperous, and the Negev and the western foothills were settled?'"

> And the word of the LORD came again to Zechariah: "This is what the LORD Almighty says: 'Administer true justice; show mercy and compassion to one another. Do not oppress the widow or the fatherless, the alien or the poor. In your hearts do not think evil of each other.'"

> "But they refused to pay attention; stubbornly they turned their backs and stopped up their ears. They made their hearts as hard as flint and would not listen to the law or to *the words*

that the LORD Almighty had sent by his Spirit through the earlier prophets. So the LORD Almighty was very angry" (Zech 7:7-12, my italics).

Here again, we notice that it is a later prophet who can speak of the role of the Spirit in the ministry of the earlier ones (a claim they so rarely made for themselves). And we also notice that the major features of the message of those earlier prophets, sent by God's Spirit, were the fundamental requirements of God's law: to do justice, to show mercy and compassion, and to reject the exploitation of the needy. This is not really very surprising. We are told that these are the very things God is most concerned about. So naturally, if the Spirit of Yahweh, the God who cares passionately about justice and compassion gets hold of somebody and compels them to speak out, what else will they speak about? The prophetic Spirit of *truth* is also the Spirit of *justice*. Truth and justice are of the very essence of the character of the God of the Bible (Is 5:16). His Spirit inevitably highlights truth and justice whenever he speaks. He could not be the Spirit of the LORD God and not speak of what the LORD God delights in and longs for. So any person who claims to speak in the name of the LORD but whose message lacks truth or is unconcerned for justice is not speaking by the LORD's Spirit.

And so we come back to the prophetic text where we began this chapter, Micah 3:8, and quote it this time in full. Micah is contrasting himself with the false prophets and their congenial message.

But as for me, I am filled with power,
   with the Spirit of the LORD,
   and with justice and might,
to declare to Jacob his transgression,
   to Israel his sin.

This verse is all the more significant precisely because, as we have seen, it is so unusual for a pre-exilic prophet to speak of the Spirit of God in relation to his own words. But when this prophet does, the connection he instantly makes is with justice. In fact the parallel structure of the second and third lines in the verse virtually equate the two. For Micah, to be filled with the *Spirit* is to be filled with *justice*, which in this context probably means "with passion for the just cause of the poor and exploited."

Why is this connection so natural that it can be stated in this directly parallel form? Because the Spirit in the Old Testament is the Spirit *of Yahweh*—the LORD, not just of any god, not just of some abstract divine impulse. And the rest of the Old Testament shows beyond all possible doubt that Yahweh, the God of Israel, is the God whose very character is the foundation of all justice, righteousness, truth and integrity. This Yahweh is on the throne of the universe, and "righteousness and justice are the foundation of his throne" (Ps 97:2). Anyone, then, who truly has the Spirit of *this* God will love what he loves, will value what he values, will care for those he cares for. In fact, nobody can even claim to know God who is not concerned for justice.

> "Let not the wise man boast of his wisdom
>   or the strong man boast of his strength
>   or the rich man boast of his riches,
> but let him who boasts boast about this:
>   that he understands and knows me,
>   that I am the LORD, who exercises kindness,
>   justice and righteousness on earth,
>   for in these I delight," declares the LORD. (Jer 9:23-24)

> "[Josiah] did righteousness and justice,
> so it went well for him.

He defended the cause of the poor and needy,
so it went well.
Is not this what it means to know me?"
declares the LORD. (Jer 22:15-16, my translation)

Here, then, is another test of whether or not some of these great, so-called prophetic ministries are truly from the Spirit of *this* God. Are they concerned about justice for the poor and needy? Or do they avoid all such issues on the grounds of "staying out of politics" (and therefore in fact endorsing the political status quo that keeps such people poor and needy)? "Staying out of politics" is precisely something the Spirit-led prophets of the Old Testament never did. It would never have occurred to them, even though they would have had a far more comfortable life if they had. But then, a comfortable life was not what a prophet expected. If the Spirit of Yahweh called you, it called for the courage to stand for justice.

CONCLUSION

What, then, have we learned in this chapter about the prophetic Spirit? We began with 2 Peter 1:20-21, and we saw that it tells us that true prophecy in the Old Testament was inspired by the Holy Spirit as "men spoke from God." That is why we believe in the inspiration of the Bible and in its double authorship—words of human beings and Word of God. But that conviction then drove us back to see *exactly what kind of word* it was that the Holy Spirit inspired the prophets to speak. And we have seen that, in contrast to the false prophets who deceived people with lies of their own devising and never challenged them about the rampant injustice in society, Spirit-filled prophets spoke the truth and stood for justice.

The same Micah who claimed the power and justice of the Spirit of the LORD also threw out the following classic challenge:

> He has shown you, O man, what is good.
> And what does the LORD require of you?
> To do justice, to love faithfulness,
> and to walk humbly with your God. (Mic 6:8, my translation)

As we seek to discern the presence or absence of the Spirit in ministries that claim to be prophetic today, we should listen to those who bring that kind of message, and whose personal and organizational lives embody it. And we should beware of false prophets who have no concern for doing justice, who love only themselves and who walk in arrogant defiance of God, no matter how much they claim the name of his Son or his Spirit.

4

The Anointing Spirit

In the last two chapters we saw the work of the Spirit of God in the Old Testament in empowering leaders, in giving the law and in enabling people to stand up for justice. Kings in Israel were supposed to embody all three of these. Kings were expected to be strong leaders in order to defend their people (like the judges), in battle if necessary. Kings were expected to know and serve the law and to give wise decisions when cases were brought before them. And most of all kings were ideally expected to provide justice for the weak and poor—especially those who lacked the natural protection of strong families to care for them, such as widows and orphans. Here are some texts that express these ideals. You will notice that they come from all over the Old Testament—the Law, the Prophets, the narratives, the psalms and the wisdom literature. The mandate and expectations on Israelite kings was extensive and well known.

> When [the king] takes the throne of his kingdom, he is to write for himself on a scroll a copy of this law, taken from that of the priests, who are Levites. It is to be with him, and he is to read it all the days of his life so that he may learn to revere the LORD his God and follow carefully all the words of this law and these decrees and not consider himself better than his brothers and turn from the law to the right or to the left. (Deut 17:18-20)

Endow the king with your justice, O God,
   the royal son with your righteousness.
He will judge your people in righteousness,
   your afflicted ones with justice. . . .
He will defend the afflicted among the people
   and save the children of the needy. . . .
For he will deliver the needy who cry out,
   the afflicted who have no one to help.
He will take pity on the weak and the needy
   and save the needy from death. (Ps 72:1, 4, 12-13)

It is not for kings, O Lemuel—not for kings to drink wine,
   not for rulers to crave beer,
lest they drink and forget what the law decrees,
   and deprive all the oppressed of their rights. . . .
Speak up for those who cannot speak for themselves,
   for the rights of all who are destitute.
Speak up and judge fairly;
   defend the rights of the poor and needy. (Prov 31:4-5, 8-9)

Hear the word of the LORD, O king of Judah, you who sit on
David's throne. . . . Do what is just and right. Rescue from the
hand of his oppressor the one who has been robbed. Do no
wrong or violence to the alien, the fatherless or the widow, and
do not shed innocent blood in this place. (Jer 22:2-3)

When all Israel heard the verdict the king [Solomon] had given,
they held the king in awe, because they saw that he had wisdom
from God to administer justice. (1 Kings 3:28)

Praise be to the LORD your God, who has delighted in you and
placed you on the throne of Israel. Because of the LORD's eternal

love for Israel, he has made you [Solomon] king, to maintain justice and righteousness. (1 Kings 10:9)

Such high expectations could not be met with human strength alone. That is why for all these responsibilities, kings needed the Spirit of the LORD God. And that is what their "anointing" symbolized. Kings in Israel were anointed with oil, speaking of the commissioning and empowering that Yahweh (the LORD) gave them through his Spirit for the tasks he laid upon them.

Anointing, then, is a sign of "office"—not in the sense of status and privilege, but rather in the sense of task and responsibility. An "anointed one" simply meant somebody chosen and commissioned by God to do a job that God wanted to be done, and then enabled by the power of God's Spirit to get on and do it. In that sense it could even apply to a non-Israelite king. Remarkably (and probably surprisingly for those who first heard it), Isaiah speaks of God referring to Cyrus, the king of Persia, in this way:

[He] says of Cyrus, "He is my shepherd
    and will accomplish all that I please;
he will say of Jerusalem, 'Let it be rebuilt,'
    and of the temple, 'Let its foundations be laid.'"

This is what the LORD says to his anointed,
to Cyrus, whose right hand I take hold of. (Is 44:28—45:1)

Cyrus could be called "the LORD's anointed one" because, as the text says, he was going to carry out what God wanted to be done, and God would strengthen and enable him to do it.

So in this chapter we shall look first of all at the anointing of the historical kings of Israel and what that meant. Then, second, we shall look at the anointing of the one whom the Old Testament anticipated as the

coming servant-king. That will mean we have to look also at the whole
mission of God through Israel, which the servant-king would be
anointed to carry out in the power of God's Spirit. Naturally enough,
that will lead us on, third, to the anointing and mission of Jesus, the
Christ (which of course means "anointed one"), who fulfilled the mission of the servant-king. And from there it is but one more step, finally,
to consider the anointing and mission of those whom Christ himself
commissioned—namely the church, including ourselves. The conti-
nuity in all this great sweep of biblical teaching is provided by the one
we are focusing on throughout this book—the Holy Spirit of God.

ANOINTING AND THE HISTORICAL KINGS

Saul. Saul was the first anointed king of Israel. You can read the story
in 1 Samuel 9—10. The relevant verses that refer to his anointing and
the role of the Spirit are as follows:

> Then Samuel took a flask of oil and poured it on Saul's head and
> kissed him, saying, "Has not the LORD anointed you leader over
> his inheritance?". . .
>
> "The Spirit of the LORD will come upon you in power, and
> you will prophesy with them; and you will be changed into a
> different person.". . .
>
> When they arrived at Gibeah, a procession of prophets met
> him; the Spirit of God came upon him in power, and he joined
> in their prophesying. (1 Sam 10:1, 6, 10)

The anointing was, on the one hand, a simple physical act. A flask
of olive oil was actually poured over Saul's head as a symbolic and
very visible gesture. But it was then followed, on the other hand, by
a spiritual anointing—an experience of the mysterious power of the
Spirit of Yahweh that clearly affected Saul very deeply and visibly.

This combination of symbolic action and internal effect had two implications in this instance. On the one hand, it authenticated the word of Samuel as a prophet—for what he had told Saul to expect actually did happen (not to mention the fact that his lost donkeys were found). And on the other hand, it initially authorized Saul himself for the leadership role into which he was about to be thrust. His early actions were clear demonstrations of the power of the Spirit of Yahweh at work in his leadership.

However, as we saw in chapter 2, in Saul's case, as with some of those who had been judges before him, this anointing did not guarantee his success as a leader or his faithfulness or his long-term effectiveness. Because of folly and disobedience, his career went from early hope to mid-term squandering to final self-destruction. Nevertheless, it is interesting that his status as "the LORD's anointed" was respected, even by David who had also been anointed to be the next king (1 Sam. 16:13). Clearly, the act of anointing and the power of the Yahweh's Spirit that went along with it was not something to be lightly disregarded, even when the one who bore it was becoming increasingly unworthy of it.

David. In the wake of Saul's failure, and even while he was grieving over it, Samuel was asked to anoint David instead.

> The LORD said to Samuel, "How long will you mourn for Saul, since I have rejected him as king over Israel? Fill your horn with oil and be on your way; I am sending you to Jesse of Bethlehem. I have chosen one of his sons to be king." (1 Sam 16:1)

After some formalities and an unexpected delay, the right son is finally found and the ceremony is completed.

> Then the LORD said, "Rise and anoint him; he is the one."

So Samuel took the horn of oil and anointed him in the presence of his brothers, and from that day on the Spirit of the LORD came upon David in power." (1 Sam 16:12-13)

In David's case, as distinct from Saul's, the anointing is met with a more wholehearted obedience to God (though not by any means with moral perfection, as we well know from the rest of his story; David was still capable of great sin). God speaks of David as "a man after my own heart" (1 Sam 13:14). This phrase almost certainly does not mean in Hebrew what it has come to sound like in English. As an idiom in English, the phrase "a man after my own heart" has come to mean someone I am particularly fond of, who shares my likings, perhaps even my favorite person. But we know that God has no special favorites in that sense. We must remember that the Hebrew word *heart* was not so much the seat of the emotions as of the will. Your emotions were located somewhat lower down the body—in your bowels. The heart, in Hebrew idiom, is where you do your thinking, weighing up, deciding and planning. So "a man after God's *heart*" means one who will think and do as God chooses, one who will carry out the plans that God has in his mind. When the phrase is first used in 1 Samuel 13:14, it stands in contrast to Saul who had failed to carry out God's commands. David is neither morally perfect nor God's special favorite. He is simply the one who will obey and accomplish where Saul had disobeyed and failed.

Saul and David, then, were both anointed as kings. But their stories show clearly that anointing by itself is no guarantee of faithfulness or even of long-term legitimacy in the service of God. Anointing must be met with obedience to God, with trust in God, with serving God and doing his will. Even for the foreign king Cyrus (who was never, of course, literally anointed as an Israelite king), this was the point. As the text above shows, whether he was ever aware of it or not, he was chosen by God to accomplish God's purpose within history, and he did so. In contrast, most of the kings of Israel, though physically anointed and fully aware of what it meant, actually failed to do what their anointing symbolized. They were anointed on their head with oil, but they were not obedient in their lives. They failed to fulfill the significance of their anointing.

It was this continuing failure of the historical kings of Israel (both in the northern kingdom of Israel and the southern kingdom of Judah) that led to increasing hopes of a coming anointed one, a coming king in the line of David, a man truly "after God's heart," who *would* be fully obedient, who would fully carry out the saving work of God in the power of God's Spirit. So we turn now to consider that figure of prophetic hope and vision.

ANOINTING AND THE COMING SERVANT-KING

Here are some of the key texts regarding the anticipated king. As you read them, consider what elements they all have in common.

> A shoot will come up from the stump of Jesse;
> from his roots a Branch will bear fruit.
> The Spirit of the LORD will rest on him—
> > the Spirit of wisdom and of understanding,
> > the Spirit of counsel and of power,
> > the Spirit of knowledge and of the fear of the LORD—
> and he will delight in the fear of the LORD.
> He will not judge by what he sees with his eyes,
> > or decide by what he hears with his ears;
> but with righteousness he will judge the needy,
> > with justice he will give decisions for the poor of the earth.
> He will strike the earth with the rod of his mouth;

with the breath of his lips he will slay the wicked.
Righteousness will be his belt
    and faithfulness the sash around his waist. (Is 11:1-5)

"Here is my servant, whom I uphold,
    my chosen one in whom I delight;
I will put my Spirit on him
    and he will bring justice to the nations.
He will not shout or cry out,
    or raise his voice in the streets.
A bruised reed he will not break,
    and a smoldering wick he will not snuff out.
In faithfulness he will bring forth justice;
    he will not falter or be discouraged
till he establishes justice on earth.
    In his law the islands will put their hope."
This is what God the LORD says—
he who created the heavens and stretched them out,
    who spread out the earth and all that comes out of it,
who gives breath to its people,
    and life to those who walk on it:
"I, the LORD, have called you in righteousness;
    I will take hold of your hand.
I will keep you and will make you
    to be a covenant for the people
    and a light for the Gentiles,
to open eyes that are blind,
    to free captives from prison
    and to release from the dungeon those who sit in darkness."
        (Is 42:1-7)

The Spirit of the Sovereign LORD is on me,
    because the LORD has anointed me
to preach good news to the poor.
    He has sent me to bind up the brokenhearted,
to proclaim freedom for the captives
    and release from darkness for the prisoners,
    to proclaim the year of the LORD's favor
    and the day of vengeance of our God,
to comfort all who mourn,
    and provide for those who grieve in Zion—
to bestow on them a crown of beauty
    instead of ashes,
the oil of gladness
    instead of mourning,
and a garment of praise
    instead of a spirit of despair. (Is 61:1-3)

I trust you noticed at least three things that these great passages from Isaiah all have in common:

They all speak of a coming one—sometimes in the language of kingship (son of David), coronation and rule; sometimes in terms of a servant.

They all speak of the role of the Spirit of Yahweh (the LORD) in relation to that person and the tasks he will carry out. He will manifestly be filled with the power of God's Spirit.

They all speak of God achieving his own mission or purpose through this servant-king—this figure who will come.

Here, then, is clearly an "anointed one" par excellence. Like the historical kings, he too will be anointed, but there is a mystery in that his kingship will be unlike most human kings we've ever known. He will be characterized by the humility and gentleness of a servant. Like the kings, his anointing will symbolize the power and presence of God's Spirit, but in his case there is detailed description of what that will include. And above all, his anointing is essentially his commissioning to carry out God's ultimate mission and purpose for the world—not just for Israel but "to the ends of the earth."

Now this is a lot to grasp all at once, even though as Christians we know it leads ultimately to Jesus Christ, our servant-king. But before we look at Jesus, we need to put all of this prophetic picture that points to him in its wider context. We need to see it in the light of the whole sweep of God's mission in the Bible. Paul speaks about "the whole counsel of God" (Acts 20:27 RSV) by which he means the whole revealed plan, purpose or mission of God that we know from the Scriptures. Paul spent three long years teaching that to the Christians in Ephesus—and now we're going to take a whirlwind tour through it in three short subheadings! We shall look at the mission of God, the mission of Israel and the mission of the Servant. Only then can we fully understand the mission of Jesus and the mission of the church. And of course we will be linking the role of the Spirit of God to all of these dimensions. And we need to start right at the beginning.

The mission of God. The Bible presents to us a God with a mission. Even in its opening pages we meet God setting about his work of creation as a dynamic mission to be accomplished. There we see God systematically thinking, planning, deciding, commanding, acting, accomplishing and evaluating. Creation is the opening mission statement of our biblical God.

When human beings appear in this story, a clear mission is also expressed. God's purpose was that these human creatures should be made in his own image, and that they should rule the earth

(Gen 1:26-28). But if they were to be like God (in his image), then they would exercise that rule through care and service (Gen 2:15). Kingship exercised through servanthood is the very nature of human relationship to creation as described in Genesis 1—2. This was God's intended pattern for life on earth. That's why he made the earth. That's why he put us in it. That was the creational mission of God.

But we blew it. We rebelled against God's authority, distrusted God's word and disobeyed God's commands (Gen 3). As a result we plunged ourselves and the earth into the chaos of sin and evil, violence and corruption, strife and suffering, that we find ourselves in still. The story of the accumulating grip of sin in the human race runs through Genesis 3—11, climaxing in the story of the tower and city of Babel in Genesis 11. There God deals with humanity as they try to act in unified arrogance. Instead, the nations now find themselves scattered in confusion over the face of the earth, which we already know stands under God's curse. It is a bleak picture indeed. What hope is there now for the mission of God in creation?

But God decided not to abandon nor to destroy his creation, but rather to redeem it. So he called Abraham, and with Abraham we enter the next major phase of the mission of God—God as redeemer.

Genesis 12 records God's call, command and promise to Abraham:

Leave your country, your people and your father's household
and go to the land I will show you.
I will make you into a great nation
    and I will bless you;
I will make your name great,
    and you will be a blessing.
I will bless those who bless you,

and whoever curses you I will curse;
and all peoples on earth
will be blessed through you. (Gen 12:1-3)

God promised three things to Abraham himself: (1) that he would
have descendants and become a great people; (2) that God would
bless this people in a special relationship which is later called a covenant; and (3) that God would give them a land to live in. These
promises provide a framework for the following major sections of the
Old Testament story, as bit by bit God fulfilled them. But the bottom
line of the covenant with Abraham widens the scope of the promise
out far beyond Israel as a nation: "through you all nations on the
earth will find blessing." The vision is universal. In fact, this promise
to Abraham in Genesis 12 is God's answer to the problems posed by
human sin in Genesis 3—11. In Genesis 11 we found the nations
scattered under God's curse. Now we hear that God's intention is that
the nations should once again be blessed, as the earth and humanity
were at creation. So Abraham is actually a fresh start for the world.
This promise is God's great manifesto. This text is God's declaration
of his mission, which is nothing less than the blessing of all nations.

So important is this promise to Abraham in the Bible that Paul actually calls it the gospel. We may have thought that the gospel begins
with Matthew, but Paul says it begins in Genesis.

Consider Abraham: "He believed God, and it was credited to
him as righteousness." Understand, then, that those who believe are children of Abraham. The Scripture foresaw that God
would justify the Gentiles by faith, and announced *the gospel in
advance* to Abraham: "All nations will be blessed through you."
So those who have faith are blessed along with Abraham, the
man of faith. (Gal 3:6-9, my italics)

The mission of God, then, is to bless all nations on earth. But how? Well, we need the whole of the rest of the Bible to answer that, including of course the New Testament. But the first part of the answer lies in Genesis also—the promise of a people. Out of Abraham's descendants, at first physical, and then also his spiritual seed, God would create a whole community of people through whom his blessing would come to the nations.

But this would need to be a different kind of people from the sinful nations already rampant on the earth. In a world that was characterized by Sodom and Gomorrah, God wanted there to be a people who would be different, people who would be committed to his ways and his values. That, God reminded himself in a conversation with Abraham, was the very reason for which he had chosen Abraham in the first place. God spoke these words at the very point when he was on his way to judge Sodom and Gomorrah:

> Abraham will surely become a great and powerful nation, and all nations on earth will be blessed through him. For I have chosen him, so that he will direct his children and his household after him to keep the way of the LORD by doing what is right and just, so that the LORD will bring about for Abraham what he has promised him. (Gen 18:18-19)

Do you see how these verses bind together some very important things? At the beginning (Gen 18:18) and at the end (last line of Gen 18:19) God reminds himself of his ultimate mission, which is blessing for all nations. But then in the middle he speaks of his choice of Abraham ("I have chosen him") and his ethical expectation on Abraham's people, Israel ("to keep the way of the LORD by doing righteousness and justice"). The whole statement is tightly bound together as a declaration of intent. God had called Abraham—why? So that he would teach his descendants to live in the way God wanted—why? So that God could fulfill his promise of blessing all the nations.

The mission of God, then, includes God's people and God's standards. God was not going to bless the nations just straight out of heaven; he would do it through a people on earth. But that community of God's mission on earth were not just to be the physical and historical means by which God would eventually send his Son to be our Savior; they had a part to play by being different, by living in the ways of the LORD. That was their mission.

The mission of Israel. The people of Israel in the Old Testament knew that God had chosen them. They were a chosen people—that was one of their most fundamental beliefs. But they were not chosen for a unique and exclusive privilege that would forever belong to them alone. No, they were chosen for a unique and inclusive responsibility which would ultimately extend to all nations on earth. Their mission was to fulfill God's mission by being the vehicle of his blessing to the nations, or—to use the language of Isaiah—to be a light to the nations that God's salvation should go to the ends of the earth. Israel in the Old Testament was not chosen *over against* the rest of the nations, but *for the sake of* the rest of the nations.

This identity and mission was given to Israel right at the start of their pilgrimage as a nation, the moment they reached Mount Sinai after the exodus. Right there, before they went any further, and before he even gave them the Ten Commandments or the rest of the law, God makes this very important statement to Israel:

> You yourselves have seen what I did to Egypt, and how I carried you on eagles' wings and brought you to myself. Now if you obey me fully and keep my covenant, then out of all nations you will be my treasured possession. Although the whole earth

is mine, you will be for me a kingdom of priests and a holy nation. (Ex 19:4-6)

The two phrases at the end of this passage express what God had
in mind for Israel. They were to be a *priestly* people and a *holy* nation.
In order to understand this, we need to remember what the priests
were in Israel. The priest stood in the middle between God and the
rest of the people. In that position he operated in both directions. On
the one hand, it was the job of the priest to teach God's law to the
people (see, e.g., Lev 10:10-11; Deut 33:10; Jer 18:18; Mal 2:7-9). So
through the priests, God would come to the people and make his way
known to them. On the other hand, it was the job of the priest to
bring the sacrifices of the people to God so that through the blood
sprinkled on the altar, their sins would be atoned for and they could
come back into fellowship with God and one another. So through the
priests, the people could come to God. The priests, then, brought
God and people together by bringing God's law to the people and
bringing the people's sacrifices to God. And then they were also entrusted with pronouncing God's blessing upon the people (Num
6:22-27).

So it is wonderfully significant that God here in Exodus 19 says to
his whole people, "You will be my priesthood among all the nations
on the earth." That is, as a whole people, you will be for the nations
what your priests are for you. You will be the people through whom
God will make himself known to the nations through the revelation
that he will give to you in his law and all the other words and Scriptures. And you will be the people through whom eventually God will
draw the nations to himself, into a forgiven, reconciled, covenant relationship. Thus, just as your priests bless you, so you will be a blessing to the nations. Now that role and identity of Israel as a "priest-

hood" for God among the nations was therefore a "missionary" task.

How was Israel to fulfill this mission? Did it mean that they were supposed to set off on missionary journeys to the other nations? I don't think so. I do not find evidence in the Old Testament itself that God ever intended Israel to *go to* the rest of the nations during that era. Occasionally an individual might be sent—as, for example, Jonah was sent to Nineveh. But on the whole, the mission of Israel was a matter of *being* rather than *going.* There was something fresh and unprecedented when Jesus after his resurrection told his disciples to go and make disciples of the nations. That was the dawn of a new era. So mission in the New Testament is mainly "centrifugal"— that is, going out from the center toward the edges—an expanding mission. This certainly involved sending people, as the church at Antioch sent Paul and Barnabas. But in the Old Testament, mission is more "centripetal"—that is, attraction toward a central point. That is part of the meaning of Israel being a light to the nations: nations would be attracted to that light, for light is by its nature attractive (cf. Is 62:1-3).

So if Israel were not meant to *go* but to *be,* what exactly were they to be? The same verse gives the answer. They were to be *holy.* Being holy fundamentally means being different or distinctive. God wanted Israel to be a model of how human life ought to be. He wanted Israel to be a society that was visibly, socially, economically, politically and religiously different from the nations around. They would be as different from the other nations in their quality of life as Yahweh, the God of Israel, was different from the gods of the other nations in his moral character. So Israel's mission was to reflect Yahweh their God in the midst of the nations—to be holy as he is holy; to be light as he is light.

In practical terms, this sense of Israel's distinctiveness was expressed often in their law. For example:

You must not do as they do in Egypt, where you used to live, and you must not do as they do in the land of Canaan, where I am bringing you. Do not follow their practices. You must obey my laws and be careful to follow my decrees. I am the LORD your God. (Lev 18:3-4)

Be holy, because I the LORD your God, am holy. (Lev 19:2)

Observe [these laws] carefully, for this will show your wisdom and understanding to the nations, who will hear about all these decrees and say, "Surely this great nation is a wise and understanding people." What other nation is so great as to have their gods near them the way the LORD our God is near us whenever we pray to him? And what other nation is so great as to have such righteous decrees and laws as this body of laws I am setting before you today? (Deut 4:6-8)

Well, it all started off with great hopes and good intentions. "Everything the LORD says, we will do," chorused the Israelites, twice over (Ex 24:3, 7; Deut 5:27). And then they went off and did everything except what the LORD said, and did many things that the LORD had specifically said they should not do. So the whole history of Israel, as it is told in the great history books of Joshua, Judges, Samuel and Kings, is one of disobedience, rebellion and failure. In fact, Israel simply replicates the story of the fall of humanity. The story of Israel is a recapitulation of the story of Genesis 1—11. Blessing, promise and command, followed by sin and rebellion. Perhaps we should not be very surprised.

So the history of Israel finally ran into the buffers of God's judgment and into the sands of exile. The northern kingdom of Israel was destroyed by Assyria and the people scattered in 721 B.C. And In 587

B.C., Nebuchadnezzar came down on Jerusalem with his Babylonian armies. The city was besieged and destroyed after terrible suffering. The temple was burned down and the king was carried off into exile along with most of the population of Judah. And all the prophets of the time interpreted these events clearly as the judgment of God.

So was it "The End"? Was their history at a full stop? Had Israel finally stepped off the stage into the graveyard of oblivion, never to rise again? Many in Israel thought so and sank into despair. But not God. Certainly it was the end for that generation, but it was not the end of God's covenant promise to his people as a whole. And it was certainly not the end of God's mission to bless the nations through this people.

The great prophecies that we sampled earlier from Isaiah were addressed to the exiles, and they spoke of hope beyond judgment. Yes, Israel was suffering God's punishment for their sin, but the time of punishment would end and God's word would be "Comfort, comfort my people" (Is 40:1). And the heart of that note of comfort and reassurance was that Israel was still God's servant, still called and chosen in Abraham, still intended to be for the blessing of "all flesh," who would ultimately see God's glory.

> But you, O Israel, my servant,
>   Jacob, whom I have chosen,
>   you descendants of Abraham my friend,
> I took you from the ends of the earth,
>   from its farthest corners I called you.
> I said, "You are my servant";
>   I have chosen you and have not rejected you.
> So do not fear, for I am with you;
>   do not be dismayed for I am your God.

I will strengthen you and help you;

    I will uphold you with my righteous right hand. (Is 41:8-10)

So there is a future for God's people. God's mission for Israel still goes on. The promise to Abraham is not dead. The nations will still be blessed.

But the massive question was, how could Israel fulfill such a mission now, given their situation? In exile, Israel was a failed servant. They were disabled and disqualified by their sin and rebellion. They were historically paralysed. This is the utterly realistic assessment of their condition. Here is the same prophet's dire description of Israel in exile:

Hear, you deaf;

    look, you blind, and see!

Who is blind but my servant,

    and deaf like the messenger I send?

Who is blind like the one committed to me,

    blind like the servant of the LORD?

You have seen many things, but have paid no attention;

    your ears are open, but you hear nothing.

It pleased the LORD

    for the sake of his righteousness

    to make his law great and glorious.

But this is a people plundered and looted,

    all of them trapped in pits

    or hidden away in prisons.

They have become plunder,

    with no one to rescue them;

they have been made loot,

    with no one to say, "Send them back." (Is 42:18-22)

The mission of God's Servant. And so, in this context of Israel as God's failing servant, God announces a new beginning, a new arrival—one who would come and embody the mission of Israel by taking it on himself. He is announced as "my Servant" or "the Servant of the LORD." The Servant of the LORD in Isaiah would have a mission *to* Israel—to restore Israel again to God—and would also embody the mission *of* Israel by bringing God's blessing to the nations. This was a task that only the unique Servant of the LORD could accomplish.

Of course, these chapters of Isaiah also prophesy the return of the exiles to Jerusalem and remarkably foretell that it will be Cyrus, king of Persia, who would achieve this by allowing them to go free (Is 44:28). And indeed that is what happened in 538 B.C. when Cyrus, after conquering Babylon, passed an edict that all the small populations in captivity in Babylon, including the Jews, were free to return to their homelands (2 Chron 36:22-23; Ezra 1:1-4). However, the political level was one thing, but the spiritual condition of Israel and the long-term purpose of God through them was quite another. Cyrus would send Israel back to Jerusalem. But only the Servant could bring Israel back to God. Cyrus would restore the fortunes of physical Israel as a nation in their own land. Only the Servant could fulfill the mission of Israel to be a light to all the nations and take God's salvation to the ends of the earth.

So we need to look carefully at this Servant figure in the prophecies of Isaiah, this anointed Servant of the LORD. For in him we will find crucial clues in our quest for knowing the Holy Spirit through the Old Testament. This Servant is said to be endowed with God's Spirit. So by looking closely at him, we will see the work of the Spirit at its most profound and transforming.

He is introduced as an individual (as distinct from the reference to Israel as God's servant in Is 41:8) for the first time in Isaiah 42:1-7, one of the texts quoted above (it would be worth reading it again at this point). Immediately we are reminded that he will have the Spirit of God upon him in order to carry out the mission entrusted to him. So the anointing power of Yahweh's Spirit, which readers of this prophecy would have associated with the power of God in the lives of the judges and kings like David, will be the hallmark of this Servant. Whatever the Servant does, God will be the one working through him. Whatever mission he has, he has received from God. Whatever he will accomplish, God will be accomplishing it through him. That is the point of being anointed with God's Spirit. It is a commitment and commissioning to do the will and purpose of God. We saw that so many of the historically anointed judges and kings lost sight of the purpose of their own anointing and went off to do their own thing, with disastrous results. *This* anointed Servant, however, will be the perfectly obedient one. By the Spirit of God he will fully accomplish what God intends. So what is that?

There are four main dimensions to the Spirit-filled mission of the Servant that we can see in Isaiah 42:1-7. Each of them deserves a chapter on its own because they are all major biblical themes, but we can only summarize them here.

1. Justice (Is 42:1, 3, 4)

This is the most repeated word in the passage—it occurs three times. The mission of the Servant is, above all, a mission to bring justice. In Old Testament terms, to do justice means putting things right. It includes putting an end to situations that are unfair, situations of exploitation and violence, and restoring those who are the victims of such behavior. It includes what we mean when we speak of "human rights." God says that the work of his Servant will ultimately bring about these things for the nations. So the mission of the Servant is very much in the public arena and ultimately international in scope. It is not just a matter of putting people right with God, or even only of putting things right for Israel. The text speaks rather of a comprehensive and universal achievement of God's justice on earth.

2. Compassion (Is 42:2-3)

Isaiah 42:2-3 stands in sharp contrast to what has been said about Cyrus, the king who would conquer and crush nations beneath his feet (Is 41). The Servant will be equally effective but without noise and violence. His will be justice with gentleness, strength with compassion. He will be filled with *my* Spirit, promises the LORD, so he will share the LORD's tenderness for the weak and vulnerable. The Servant's mission will be successful, but not coercive. His method will not be to solve the problem of the weak and poor by eliminating them but by restoring them in compassionate justice.

3. Enlightenment (Is 42:7)

The Servant will bring light and sight to the eyes of those in darkness and blindness. In the immediate context, this was a word of hope for Israel, who were "blind" and in the darkness of exile. But in the wider horizon of this Servant's global mission, it must include bringing enlightenment to all who live in the darkness of sin without the light of the revelation of God's saving love.

4. Liberation (Is 42:7)

Again, this would originally have brought joy to the exiles, to know that their Babylonian prison would finally be opened to set them free. But it is the language used of God's liberating intention for human beings in all forms of oppression and bondage, not least to the sin and rebellion that lies at the root of all human suffering.

All of these were important and resonant words for the exiles, to whom the prophet's words were first addressed. But the scope of the Servant's Spirit-filled mission, we have been told, goes beyond Israel to the nations. The Servant will bring the blessing of God's justice to the nations—which echoes the Abrahamic mission of Israel itself.

So, in Isaiah 49:1-6 the Servant speaks and addresses the nations in his own right. He tells how God has given him a mission which has two clear parts.

> Listen to me, you islands;
>> hear this, you distant nations:
> Before I was born the LORD called me;
>> from my birth he has made mention of my name. . . .
>
> He said to me, "You are my servant,
>> Israel, in whom I will display my splendor."
> But I said, "I have labored to no purpose;
>> I have spent my strength in vain and for nothing.
> Yet what is due me is in the LORD's hand,
>> and my reward is with my God."
> [5] And now the LORD says—
>> he who formed me in the womb to be his servant
> to bring Jacob back to him
>> and gather Israel to himself,
> for I am honored in the eyes of the LORD
>> and my God has been my strength—
> [6] he says:
> "It is too small a thing for you to be my servant
>> to restore the tribes of Jacob
>> and bring back those of Israel I have kept.

I will also make you a light for the Gentiles,

that you may bring my salvation to the ends of the earth."
    (Is 49:1, 3-6)

Notice the transition that takes place between Isaiah 49:5 and Isaiah 49:6. The Servant's mission is to restore Israel to God. But, God says, that is not all. That is not nearly enough. In addition to his mission to Israel, God's long-range purpose for his Servant is to bring God's salvation to the ends of the earth! Also notice carefully that this mission of the Servant to the nations is *in addition to,* not *instead of,* his mission of restoring Israel. Mission to the nations is an extension of the mission to Israel, not a replacement of it. So the Servant, then, has a mission *to Israel.* And yet, he also embodies the mission *of Israel* by being commissioned to take the blessing of God's salvation to the nations.

But this mission of the Servant will be costly. The verses we have just read in Isaiah 49 speak of frustration and struggle. The next time the Servant speaks, it is to describe his experience of rejection, contempt and physical abuse (Is 50:6). And the climactic Servant passage, Isaiah 52:13—53:12 describes how the Servant will suffer a travesty of justice in which he is finally executed with great violence. Yet through that death, as a self-sacrifice, God's saving purpose will be accomplished. For God will lay on his Servant the sin of us all, and by his death he will enable many to be counted righteous. The Servant, says our prophet, *will accomplish* all God's purpose, but it will be at the cost of his own life. Yet through paying that ultimate price, the Servant will experience victory and vindication from God, and finally be glorified.

See my servant will act wisely;

he will be raised and lifted up and highly exalted. . . .

But he was pierced for our transgressions,
>   he was crushed for our iniquities;
> the punishment that brought us peace was upon him,
>   and by his wounds we are healed.
> We all, like sheep, have gone astray,
>   each of us has turned to his own way;
> and the LORD has laid on him
>   the iniquity of us all. . . .

> After the suffering of his soul
>   he will see the light of life and be satisfied;
> by his knowledge my righteous servant will justify many,
>   and he will bear their iniquities. (Is 52:13; 53:5-6, 11)

Finally, in Isaiah 61:1-2 this Servant (for almost certainly these are the Servant's own words) speaks again, in language that echoes our first passage (Is 42). "Here I am," he says. "This is what I came to do. This is what the Spirit of the LORD has anointed me to do."

> The Spirit of the Sovereign LORD is on me,
>   because the LORD has anointed me
>   to preach good news to the poor.
> He has sent me to bind up the brokenhearted,
>   to proclaim freedom for the captives
>   and release from darkness for the prisoners,
> to proclaim the year of the LORD's favor
>   and the day of vengeance of our God,
> to comfort all who mourn. (Is 61:1-2)

Did you notice again the same claim to the anointing of the Spirit of God? And the same multitasking description of his mission? And did you recognize here a word that brings us very close to our next step—namely to Jesus himself with these words on his lips in a synagogue in Nazareth one Sabbath morning?

But just before we jump the centuries to Jesus, let's pause to look back over what we have discovered so far. We have seen the *mission of God*—which is to bless all nations on earth. We have seen the *mission of Israel*—which was to be the vehicle of that blessing to the nations, as promised to Abraham. But in the context of Israel's historical failure, we have seen the *mission of the Servant of the* LORD—a dual mission of restoring Israel and also bringing justice, compassion, enlightenment and liberation to the ends of the earth. All this was prophesied with Israel still in exile.

Well, the exile came to an end in 538 B.C. Or did it? Yes, many (though by no means all) Jews returned from Babylon to Judah, rebuilt Jerusalem and eventually the temple also. But the centuries passed and Israel seemed to be still under the heel of foreign oppressors—initially the Persians, then the Greeks and finally the Romans. In heart and spirit they felt like exiles even in their own land. They felt unforgiven, unliberated and oppressed, as though they were still in captivity. And so they continued to long for deliverance, for true liberation. They took up these prophecies again, knowing that of course they had been partially fulfilled in the remarkable release from Babylon and return to their own land, and yet knowing also that they spoke of something greater and more magnificent yet to come. They longed for the One who would come and achieve all that God had promised. They longed for the Anointed One, the one on whom God's Spirit would rest, the one who would bring in the longed for age of God's unhindered rule and the end of the domination of their enemies.

ANOINTING AND THE MISSION OF JESUS, THE CHRIST

And so it was, then, that on a Sabbath morning in a dusty synagogue in Nazareth, in the backwaters of despised Galilee, a thirty-year-old local villager took his turn to read from the scroll of the Prophets. Jesus read these words that we have since numbered and labelled as Isaiah 61:1-2. Then he sat down. That was the customary posture for explaining the Scriptures. What might the people have expected in a "sermon" on that text? Probably they would have expected Jesus to comment on the text in the way it had always been expounded. They would have expected to hear it in the way they had always heard it, that is, with the longing ears of a patiently suffering and long awaiting people. "What we have just read is what God has promised us," they might have expected to hear Jesus reaffirm. "The prophet tells us that this is the one we pray for. This is the one we hope for. This is the one who will come to our rescue in the power of God's Spirit like the judges of old. May your anointed one come soon, O LORD! May he even come tomorrow."

But Jesus shatters that weary assumption with words that must have electrified them all. "Today," he quietly begins, "TODAY this Scripture is being fulfilled! Right here among you, as you listen to *me!*"

Jesus claims the prophetic text as his own. Jesus makes himself the embodied sermon. And in doing so, Jesus makes the mission of God, the mission of Israel and the mission of the Servant his own mission. As the astonished people listen, the emphatic scriptural word *"me"* is no longer merely the unidentified voice of an expected One, speaking out of the ancient text of a dusty scroll. It has now become the living and very identifiable voice of one of their own young adults from their own town, speaking out of the preacher's chair in their own synagogue. Jesus ben-Joseph, son of the village carpenter, dares to claim, "The Spirit of the LORD is upon *me*; the LORD has anointed *me*."

Through this text Jesus sets out the manifesto of his own mission.

Through this text Jesus answers in advance the questions that became more and more insistent as his ministry gathered pace. "Who are you? What do you think you are doing? Why do you feel compelled to act in this way? Why are you no longer minding your own business in your father's carpenter's shop? What is the power by which you do these things?" And Jesus answers: "I have been anointed by no less than the Spirit of the LORD God himself, and this text sets out the contours of the mission of God that I am to fulfill."

But if Jesus is the one anointed by the Spirit of God, what should we expect to find in his life and ministry? Knowing the Holy Spirit through the Old Testament, we should find exactly what we do find—namely that those same four key marks of the anointed Servant of the LORD spelled out in the Old Testament are combined also in the ministry of Jesus.

There was *justice*. That was implicit in his announcement of the reign of God, which all Jesus' contemporaries knew from their Scriptures would bring God's justice to the world. Justice would mean God putting things right, and that is what Jesus went about doing in his personal relationships and teaching. It did not happen in the form of a violent revolution such as some of his supporters wanted. And it did not happen all at once, for the kingdom of God is like a seed growing secretly, or like yeast slowly permeating the dough. But it was a key element in what he taught his disciples to seek. "Blessed are those who hunger and thirst for justice," he said. "Seek first the kingdom of God and his justice" (Mt 5:6; 6:33, my translation).

There was *compassion*. Jesus sought out all those whom society rejected and marginalized, and ministered especially to them: the sick, women, children, the morally and politically compromised (prostitutes and tax collectors), Gentiles, "sinners." He even gained a reputation for such behavior. "Friend of sinners," they called him. They meant it as an insult, but Jesus took it as a compliment, for it summarized exactly why he came.

There was *enlightenment*. Teaching, teaching, always teaching—that's the picture of Jesus we see in the Gospels. Jesus certainly opened the eyes of the physically blind, but on an even greater scale he opened the eyes of the spiritually blind to the truth about God, about sin, judgment and forgiveness, about himself and the significance of his coming in relation to the story of Israel, about how life was to be lived by those who submitted to the reign of God.

There was *liberation*. Jesus went about delivering people: from sickness, from the chains of paralysis, from the burden of sin, from the loneliness of ritual exclusion, from demonic oppression, from the prison of remorse. And of course, as he put it himself, he came ultimately to give his life "as a ransom for many," thus achieving ultimate liberation for sinners.

But the Gospels show us that Jesus not only fulfilled the task of the Servant in the power of the Spirit, he also accepted the fate of the Servant, as prophesied in Isaiah. And that was to suffer rejection, contempt, unjust trial and bloody execution. And in doing all this, he took upon himself the deepest cause of all injustice, cruelty, blindness and bondage—namely our sinful rebellion against God. So Jesus went to the cross, and the cross was the cost of all those dimensions of God's mission as itemized in the mission of the Servant. And yet, although this Servant-mission led him finally to the cross, the process began even on that Sabbath in Nazareth when the people, offended by his claims and his unfavorable contrast between their hard refusal to accept him and the blessing God had brought to Gentile outsiders in the Old Testament (the widow of Zarephath and Naaman the Syrian), hustled him off for an abortive lynching.

ANOINTING AND THE MISSION OF THE CHURCH

So at last we come to our final step. We are those who claim to follow Jesus. We claim to be filled with the same Holy Spirit. And these are not arrogant claims, for they stand upon clear New Testament statements and promises. But if so, what kind of effect should the presence of the Holy Spirit have in our lives and ministry?

To put it more simply, what is "the anointing"? This is a phrase that is much used in some Christian circles. In itself it is a curious abbreviation and easily misunderstood. We ought to talk more fully of "the anointing of the Holy Spirit," since the term "the anointing," when it is used on its own these days, sometimes seems to mean little more than a powerful personality or a particularly spectacular way of speaking and ministering. As applied to preachers in some Christian cultures, it seems to be equated with plenty of noise. The greater the volume of shouting, the more proof there is that the preacher has "the anointing." This seems a long way from the anointing of the Servant of the Lord, for whom the proof of the Spirit of God was precisely that he achieved his mission but did not "shout or cry out or raise his voice in the streets." In Uganda, during a preaching seminar there, I preached several expositions of the Bible as models that were then evaluated by the participants. One participant's written comment is my favorite. "I could feel the sweet flow of the Spirit without noising up." This encouraged me, not only to be reminded that I didn't have to shout and jump around just to prove the Holy Spirit was speaking through the message, but also that the participant had realized (as an apparent surprise) that anointing is not a matter of decibels.

No, anointing by the Spirit, we have now clearly seen from the Bible, is not primarily an external thing that proves its presence by noise (though of course the Spirit of God can make a great deal of noise on occasion, as on the day of Pentecost). Rather, spiritual anointing is primarily an equipping for mission, a commissioning for service. Anointing by God's Spirit is what enables people to do what God wants to get done. And for us who follow Jesus, anointing is enabling us to do what the Scriptures have shown so clearly that God wants to get done. Mission for us has to be *mission in Christ's way*, and that means following the pattern of Spirit-filled servanthood that characterized him.

Now of course Jesus was unique. His life was unique. He was *the* Servant of the LORD—the only perfectly obedient one. His death was unique, for he was the only perfect embodiment of the living God in a human life—the unique God-man. And so he alone could take our sin upon himself in such a way that "God was in Christ reconciling the world to himself." Nobody else ever has done, ever could do, or ever needs to do what Jesus alone has done as the Son and Servant of the living God in the power of God's Spirit. In all these ways Jesus uniquely and perfectly fulfilled the mission of God for the salvation of the world.

Yes, but in another sense, Jesus passed on that mission of God to his disciples. The risen Jesus proclaimed his own universal Lordship as the foundation for mandating his disciples to replicate themselves by spreading communities of obedient discipleship throughout all the nations (Mt 28:18-20). For that task he specifically empowers them by the Holy Spirit (Lk 24:45).

> You will receive power when the Holy Spirit comes on you; and you will be my witnesses in Jerusalem, and in all Judea and Samaria, and to the ends of the earth. (Acts 1:8)

So Jesus entrusts to us, to us who stand at the end of the line of this great survey of the biblical story, the mission of God (to bless the nations of humanity), the mission of Israel (to be a light to the nations and the agent of blessing), the mission of the Servant (to bring salvation to the ends of the earth), and his own mission (that repentance and forgiveness of sins should be preached in his name—see Lk 24:47). The church is now the inheritor and agent of all these dimensions of the great biblical mission—and especially the servant mission.

This is how Paul saw his own mission. He was called to be the apostle to the nations (Gentiles), but in that task Paul saw simply the continuation of the mission of God's anointed Servant. So in Romans 15:8-9 he describes how the Messiah (Christ) became a servant of *Israel* so that the gospel could go to *the nations*. And in Acts 13:47, he explicitly quotes the Isaiah texts and applies that servant task and responsibility to himself and his small band of church-planting missionaries.

So, in line with Paul, we need to see that the mission of the Spirit-anointed Servant to the nations becomes ours too. We too need to be committed to the same holistic mission as the Servant of Isaiah 42, Isaiah 61 and Luke 4. For it is clear that in his own earthly lifetime Jesus did not "complete" the tasks of bringing justice, enlightenment and liberation to the ends of the earth. These same tasks are ours. And they call for the same combination of spiritual and physical, personal and social, historical and eternal dimensions as they did in his own ministry. For it is in *all* of these that the good news of the gospel is to be heard, applied and lived out.

Historically the church has indeed seen its mission in these broad terms. It is not a matter of engaging in *both* the gospel *and* social action, as if Christian social action was something separate from the gospel itself. The gospel has to be demonstrated in word and deed. Biblically, the gospel includes the totality of all that is good news from

God for all that is bad news in human life—in every sphere. So, like Jesus, authentic Christian mission has included good news for the poor, compassion for the sick and suffering, justice for the oppressed, liberation for the enslaved. The gospel of the Servant of God in the power of the Spirit of God addresses every area of human need and every area that has been broken and twisted by sin and evil. And the heart of the gospel, in all of these areas, is the cross of Christ.

CONCLUSION

What then is anointed mission? If it is anointed by the Spirit of God, then it will be mission that reflects the one who quoted the Old Testament and said "The Spirit of the Lord is upon me, because the Lord has anointed me . . ." If it is to be mission in the way of Christ, then it will be mission in the way of the One who unquestionably knew the Holy Spirit through the Old Testament.

There is a bracelet that carries the letters WWJD. It is meant to remind its wearers of the slogan "What Would Jesus Do?" as a way of facing everything in life from the perspective of that question. I think if you had given one to Luke, he would have changed the letters to WDJD—"What *Did* Jesus Do?" and then asked you to read on.

Filled with the Holy Spirit (as Luke stresses often), Jesus ate and drank with the poor and the marginalized, fed the hungry, talked with children, taught the crowds, comforted the bereaved, restored the ostracized, released the demon-oppressed, challenged the rich and the authorities, brought people forgiveness of sins, healed relationships as well as bodies, and in all of this declared that God reigns—here and now, and still to come. And all of this was part of *his* anointed mission.

"The Spirit of the Lord is upon *me*," he said, "for the Lord has anointed *me*." Yes, but he also said, "'As the Father has sent me, I am sending *you*.' And with that he breathed on them and said, 'Receive the Holy Spirit'" (Jn 20:21-22).

Mission in the way of Christ, then, is mission that is empowered by the anointing Spirit of God, committed to the justice and compassion of God, characterized by the Servant of God, including even suffering and the way of the cross. Before we pray so glibly (for ourselves or others) for the anointing of the Spirit, perhaps it would be good to remind ourselves what the Bible says that will mean.

5

The Coming Spirit

Our exploration of the work of the Holy Spirit in the Old Testament has opened up some very broad horizons so far. We have seen how the Israelites recognized the Spirit of Yahweh, their God:

- in creating the universe and sustaining all life on earth
- in powerful leadership, yet exercised humbly in Moses
- in the words of the prophets who courageously stood for truth and justice
- in the anointing of their kings and in the expectation of a truly anointed one to come

But as Old Testament believers looked forward through the eyes of their prophets and indeed through the hopes of their worship songs, they longed for a new era of the unhindered, unchallenged reign of Yahweh, the LORD God of Israel. That is, they wanted to see as a reality what they affirmed by faith—the kingdom of God (as the New Testament calls it). And a very significant part of that expectation was that when God fully established his reign over his people and over the earth, there would be a fresh and unprecedented outpouring of God's Spirit. This, they believed, would be one of the clearest signs of the arrival of the new age of salvation and blessing—it would be the era of God's Spirit. This did not mean, of course, that they thought the Spirit of God was not present already. Our study so far has shown just how much the Israelites did indeed know about the Spirit of God and exactly how they thought of his activities. But this future coming of the Spirit would be more than anything hitherto known, and would have some life-changing, history-changing, earth-changing effects. The creating, empowering, prophetic, anointing Spirit whom they already knew was also the coming Spirit for whom they longed. And it is this future longing for the coming of the Spirit of God (sometimes called the "eschatological" vision of the Old Testament) that leads directly on to its fulfillment at Pentecost and the great teaching of the New Testament about the Holy Spirit in relation to Jesus Christ.

So let us look at three passages in the prophets that describe the coming Spirit and the amazing effects that they anticipate—one from Isaiah, one from Ezekiel and one from Joel.

Re-creation and Righteousness: Isaiah 32

Like so many of the chapters in Isaiah, this one mixes words of imminent judgment on the people of the prophet's own day in Jerusalem with words of future hope. It begins with the bold affirmation that one day there will be a truly righteous king reigning over the people (in contrast to the degenerate dynasty that occupied the throne of David at the time).

See a king will reign in righteousness and rulers will rule with justice. (Is 32:1)

This, as we have seen, is an essential part of Israel's hope and faith—that an ideal king would do what their historical kings were anointed, but lamentably failed, to do.

Later in the chapter, that age of righteous rule is further described as an outpouring of God's Spirit in such a way that everything is transformed by it. Remember that the Spirit of God in Old Testament thought is connected with creation, with justice and with the exercise of power for the benefit of society. In this passage all three realms are affected, as they are flooded and washed by the outpoured Spirit.

> Till the Spirit is poured upon us from on high,
> > and the desert becomes a fertile field,
> > and the fertile field seems like a forest.
> Justice will dwell in the desert
> > and righteousness live in the fertile field.
> The fruit of righteousness will be peace;
> > the effect of righteousness will be quietness and confidence
> > > forever.
> My people will live in peaceful dwelling places,
> > in secure homes,
> > in undisturbed places of rest. (Is 32:15-18)

The *created order* (Is 32:15) will be renewed and restored to its full fertility and growth. The Spirit who is already constantly at work sustaining and renewing creation (Ps 104; see chapter 1), will then do so in full abundance and all nature will be transformed by his power and presence. The picture given here of the effects on creation of the outpouring of the Spirit are a condensed form of longer and more graphic descriptions of the new creation later in the book of Isaiah. Read especially Isaiah 65:17-25. Perhaps only poetry can express what lies beyond our imagination. William Cowper, the author of some familiar Christian hymns, composed a lengthy poem, of which the following lines catch something of Isaiah's vision:

> Rivers of gladness water all the earth,
> And clothe all climes with beauty. The reproach

Of barrenness is past. The fruitful field
Laughs with abundance; and the land, once lean
Or fertile only in its own disgrace,
Exults to see its thistly curse repeal'd.
The various seasons woven into one,
And that one season an eternal spring,
The garden fears no blight, and needs no fence,
For there is none to covet, all are full.
The lion, and the libbard, and the bear,
Graze with the fearless flocks. . . .

One song employs all nations; and all cry,
"Worthy the Lamb, for He was slain for us!"
The dwellers in the vales and on the rocks
Shout to each other, and the mountain tops
From distant mountains catch the flying joy;
Till, nation after nation taught the strain,
Earth rolls the rapturous Hosanna round.[1]

The *moral order* (Is 32:16) will be set right once again. The out-pouring of the Spirit—who is, as we saw in chapter three, the Spirit of justice—will inevitably mean that the very character of God will pervade the universe. Righteousness and justice are two of the biggest words in the whole ethical vocabulary of the Old Testament. They are not merely things that we are supposed to do in human life (though they certainly are that, of course). They define the order of the universe under God's rule, for, as Psalm 97:2 puts it, they are the foundation of God's throne. So when the Spirit is poured out, then

---

[1]William Cowper, "The Task," book 6, lines 763-74, 791-97, in *The Complete Poetical Works of William Cowper, Esq,* ed. Rev. A. M. H. Stebbing (New York: D. Appleton, 1856), pp. 344-45. "Libbard" probably means leopard.

God's own moral character will prevail, and will once again flood the whole of creation.

It is worth noting that Isaiah 32:16 sets justice and righteousness in the desert and in the fertile field. Righteousness and justice apply not only to the social world of human relationships (that is what immediately follows in Is 32:17), but also to the created environment in which we live—whether the uncultivated wilderness or the cultivated lands of human occupation. These too are places where justice is needed, for they are both the victims of vast and vicious injustice at human hands. The Spirit who created and sustains the earth also longs for it to be treated with justice and righteousness. And this vision looks forward to the day when it finally will be.

The *social order* (Is 32:17-18) will be restored to *shalom*. This beautiful word in Isaiah 32:17 speaks of human society enjoying the fruit of justice, which means the end of all violence, fear and dislocation because of the absence of all the things that produce them. In their place comes rest, security, confidence and well-being. All this too the prophet sees as the result of the outpouring of the Spirit.

So then, in the long gaze of the prophet, all these things will come about when the Spirit is poured out from on high. As with so many of the words of the prophets, we have to allow for the "telescopic" nature of a vision like this. Yes, we know that the Spirit was poured out on the day of Pentecost. But all these full effects of the Spirit's flood lie ahead of us yet. It is similar to what the New Testament teaches about the kingdom of God. It was indeed inaugurated by Jesus in his earthly lifetime. And yet we still look for its complete realization at his return. We still pray, "Your kingdom come, your will be done on earth as it is in heaven." There is an "already but not yet" about the kingdom of God. In the same way, we have received the firstfruits of the Holy Spirit or in Paul's metaphor, the "down-payment" or guarantee (Eph 1:13-14). But we still long and pray, as Romans 8:18-27 reminds us, for the completion of God's work of cosmic renewal, the new creation and the ultimate reign of God in righteousness and peace.

RENEWAL AND RESURRECTION: EZEKIEL 36—37

Ezekiel knew a thing or two about the Spirit of God. It was the Spirit, he tells us, that on several occasions had literally lifted him up and carried him around the place—sometimes (it would seem) in physical reality and sometimes in his visions—once even by the hair of his head (see Ezek 2:2; 3:12, 14, 24; 8:3; 11:24; 37:1).

Ezekiel lived among the exiles in Babylon. He was among those who had been deported by Nebuchadnezzar in 597 B.C. Ten years later, Nebuchadnezzar went on to destroy the city and burn the temple in 587 B.C., and a whole new flood of captives from Judah joined Ezekiel and the other exiles languishing in their "grave" (for that is what they called it, as we shall see). They thought it was all over. But was it? God had apparently become the enemy of his own people. By his graphic acted prophecies, Ezekiel made it clear that it was the hand of their own God, Yahweh, who was wielding the sword of Nebuchadnezzar. Was it really the end for the nation of Israel? Could there be any hope for the future? It seems that for the first few years, the first group of exiles with Ezekiel were optimistic about going home soon, since the city and temple were still standing. But once the Babylonian armies stormed the walls of Jerusalem, the hopes of the people lay buried in the smouldering rubble of the city and the temple. "We might as well be dead," they said. "We are nothing more than dry bones here in exile, with no life, no hope, no future." And they were right. There was no hope at all—from their side. Israel had sinned itself to the graveyard of history.

But they reckoned without God. The message of the prophets, especially Jeremiah and Ezekiel (who both witnessed the exile) and the great chapters of Isaiah 40—55 that address the exiles, was that the same God who had driven them from his land in anger at their persistent sin and rebellion for generations would eventually bring them back from exile to their own land again. And he did in 538 B.C. when Babylon itself fell to the Persians and King Cyrus passed a decree that released small captive communities like the people of Judah to return to their homelands. The return from exile was the immediate historical fulfillment of so many of the prophetic predictions that God would gather his scattered people and restore them to their own land again.

But Ezekiel sees beyond the physical restoration of the people of Judah to their little territory round Jerusalem. Like the other prophets, he saw an even greater restoration of the people to God himself and also that this required an even deeper work of grace in the hearts and wills of the people. They needed not merely political liberation and geographical relocation. They needed a radical heart transplant. In fact, they needed nothing short of resurrection. And both would be the work of the coming Spirit of God. We need to look at two passages where Ezekiel describes the work of the Spirit in these breathtaking (or perhaps better, breath-giving) transformations.

Ezekiel 36:25-27.

I will sprinkle clean water on you, and you will be clean; I will cleanse you from all your impurities and from all your idols. I will give you a new heart and put a new spirit in you; I will remove from you your heart of stone and give you a heart of flesh. And I will put my Spirit in you and move you to follow my decrees and be careful to keep my laws.

This is one of my favorite passages in the book of Ezekiel, and indeed in the Bible. It presents the gospel of God's grace in such graphic categories and is the nearest you get in the Old Testament to regeneration by the Spirit. It begins (in Ezek 36:24), as the prophets habitually do, on the plane of anticipated history—the return of Israel to the land at the end of the exile. But it moves quickly beyond anything that ever perfectly characterized the returned exiles in their postexilic history. It speaks of spiritual reality with ethical results. It speaks of cleansing and moral transformation, of radical inward change and radical outward obedience. It is, in short, a very rich word about what God alone can do through his Spirit. Knowing the Holy Spirit through the Old Testament could not be more profound, or more prophetic of Christ's work, than this.

It can only begin, of course, with the cleansing and forgiving work of God. That is a matter of pure grace and has to be an act of God. We cannot cleanse ourselves, but God promises to do so in Ezekiel 36:25. However, that is only the start. Ezekiel saw that Israel's sin (and ours) lies much deeper than either ritual uncleanness or even merely external actions. And so he goes on to describe the work of the Spirit of God in the very depths of our being.

> The problem lay not just in Israel's behaviour, but in the source of their behaviour—the attitudes and mentality that characterized them. In short, the problem was in their 'heart' and 'spirit'.
>
> The two terms heart (lēb), and spirit (rûaḥ) describe the inner human person. In Hebrew idiom, the heart is the locus of the mind, not primarily of the emotions. It is in or with the heart that a person thinks, decides and wills. The spirit reflects the inner feelings and aspirations of the person—again, not merely in the sense of emotions, but in terms of the attitude, disposition

and motivation which one brings to choices and actions. The two terms are closely related, but not identical. Israel will have to *think* differently, and *feel* differently. Their whole inner world needs to be transformed.

No longer was it enough to expect God to 'circumcise their hearts' in the graphic metaphor of Deuteronomy 30:6 (cf. Jer ·4:4). Much more radical surgery is needed now. So . . . God proposes a heart transplant. He will remove the *heart of stone*, which has made Israel hard, cold, unresponsive and dead to God's words of command or of appeal. And he will implant in its place *a heart of flesh*—flesh which is living, warm and soft, and which, in Hebrew idiom, speaks of close kinship and intimate relationship. God will transform Israel's whole mindset and fundamental orientation of will, desire and purpose.

The purpose of such transformation is wholehearted obedience. But that requires a further action of God upon Israel. '*I will put my Spirit in you.*' . . . And the effect of that will be that Israel will at last be obedient. . . . The paradox here is that God himself, by the gift of his Spirit, will see to it that his renewed people actually will fulfil the condition that he himself sets.[2]

God demands obedience. The Spirit of God enables the obedience that God demands. This is the wonderful promise of this text.

A similar paradox is found in Deuteronomy 30:1-10 (on which Ezekiel may well be reflecting here). There, in verses 2 and 10 (cf. 6:5), the fundamental command that Israel should love God with all their heart and soul is echoed in the condition that they must turn to him and obey him with all their heart and

---

[2]Christopher J. H. Wright, *The Message of Ezekiel*, The Bible Speaks Today (Downers Grove, Ill.: InterVarsity Press, 2003), pp. 296-97.

soul. Yet in the very centre of the passage (v. 6), God promises that he, the LORD your God himself, 'will circumcise your hearts and the hearts of your descendants, *so that* you may love him with all your heart and with all your soul, and live'. God will do in and for Israel what Israel's history so gloomily demonstrated they could not do for themselves. God's grace will give what God's law requires. The gospel is already breathing through such texts in the law—as it is here in Ezekiel's prophecy.

There is, of course, a tension here (as throughout the Bible) between the role of human will and choice and the role of divine causation. God commands obedience and we must make our free choice to respond and obey—or not. But at the same time, God gives his Spirit and 'makes' that obedience happen. One pole of the tension affirms human freedom. The other affirms divine sovereignty. No amount of theology will ever be able to provide a complete correlation of both truths which does not leave us still conscious of mysteries somewhere beyond our grasp. Ultimately, the proof and the test come through experience.[3]

And that seems to be what Paul comes down to when reflecting on the role of the Spirit in relation to the law in actual practical experience of Christian living in Romans 8. The Spirit (which he significantly calls "the Spirit of life") sets us free from the law at one level—in relation to sin and death and the inability of our fallen human nature to obey God. Yet the very purpose for which Christ died, and for which we are granted the indwelling Spirit, is "in order that the righteous requirements of the law might be fully met in us, who do not live according to the sinful human nature

---

[3]Ibid., p. 297.

["flesh"] but according to the Spirit" (Rom 8:1-4).

Paul almost certainly had Ezekiel in mind as he wrote this, proving that the Spirit Paul knew through the risen Christ was the same Spirit whom he knew from his Old Testament Scriptures—and the same Spirit whom we can know in the same twofold way, through Christ and the Scriptures.

Ezekiel 37:1-14. Thorough washing and a heart transplant—such are the wonderful promises connected with the coming of the Spirit in the section we have just read. But such actions, though possibly cosmetic, are not particularly helpful if performed on a corpse. And that is how the exiles felt—dead. As dead as dry bones. Look at what they were saying about themselves: "Our bones are dried up and our hope is gone; we are cut off" (Ezek 37:11). So God has to come up with an even more powerful solution. Nothing short of bringing the people back from the grave will be enough. Can God really do that? Can the Spirit of God give life to the dead? "Can these bones live?"

Ezekiel is given the answer in a vision that is probably the one thing most people remember about him—the valley of dry bones and the mesmerizing mental picture of them all coming together, bone to bone, growing back their soft tissues, and then rising in unison to life as a great army of soldiers. No horror movie could produce more graphic and startling special effects than the way Ezekiel tells his vision. And no passage of Scripture, short of the actual resurrection of Jesus himself, more powerfully portrays the sovereign Holy Spirit of God—"the Lord and Giver of life." Here again we are privileged to learn something of the power of the Holy Spirit through the Old Testament.

Ezekiel's graphic vision of dry bones is a picture of how the exiles thought of themselves—that is, as good as dead. Ezekiel first of all hears God's astounding questions, "Can these bones live?" Ezekiel would not have doubted God's power to revive the dead (there were stories in the Scriptures to that effect), but surely only when there was a body to revive soon after death, not when all that was left were bleached bones. But then, in remarkably courageous obedience, Ezekiel, in his vision, "preached" to the bones, so that the flesh came back upon them. That is itself was an amazing miracle of reversal, but what advantage has a lifeless corpse over a lifeless skeleton? No breath, no life, no hope. It is at that crucial point in the vision that the Spirit-breath of God arrives on the scene.

Then suddenly, into the continuing silence of death, the divine voice speaks for the third time, to initiate the second and final part of the momentous revival: 'Prophecy to the breath . . . "Come from the four winds, O breath, and breathe into these slain, that they may live"' (9). At this point it is worth noting the dominance of this whole scene by the Hebrew word here translated breath. It is the word *rûaḥ*, and it is used ten times in this single section (36:1-14), but with a wonderful variety of significance. At the beginning and end of the section it refers unmistakeably to the Spirit of Yahweh which had lifted Ezekiel and *set* him in the valley (1), and would eventually also lift the whole people and *settle* (same word) them back in their own land (14). But the word also means 'breath' in a literal, straightforward sense, and this is its meaning in verses 5, 6, 8 and 10. *rûaḥ* also means "wind" – powerfully moving air—and this too is found in verse 9, where *from the four winds* means, 'from all directions of the earth'. The central use, in verse 9, *O breath*, which Ezekiel is commanded to summon by prophetic word, has the ambiguity that it doubtless means the Spirit of the living God, but also accomplishes the miraculous act of artificial respiration by which the corpses begin literally to breathe again and stand up alive and vigorous as an army. So the whole scene, then, is permeated by the various activities of *rûah*—human, natural and divine: breath, wind and Spirit. And the single total effect of all this activity of *rûah* is life, life out of utter deadness.

There is another event being mirrored here. The picture of the divine breath breathing into inanimate bodies so that they come to life undoubtedly recalls the original creation of humanity as recorded in Genesis 2:7. In that account also there is a two-stage process of divine activity. First God fashioned the human creature out of the lifeless dust of the earth. At a biological level we share the same stuff and substance as the rest of creation, animal, vegetable and mineral. But then, in an act of tender intimacy, God breathed into human nostrils the breath of life[4] so that the human became a living being—living because breathing. So here in Ezekiel's vision, the unique, life-giving power of the creator God once more breathes life into inert human flesh and brings forth a miracle of new existence. The revival of Israel will be nothing less than the re-creation of humanity—a thought we must return to. . . .

When we seek to understand Ezekiel's message in its own context, it is vital to remember that his main point was to bring hope *to Israel as a people*. His vision and its interpretation was not intended to teach a doctrine of individual bodily resurrection, but to compare the restoration of Israel to the imaginary bringing back to life of the bones of a massive army of slain soldiers. The language is symbolic and metaphorical, and its application was for the still living, not the already dead. That is, Ezekiel's vision promised the exiles still alive in Babylon that there would be a living future for Israel in the return from exile; it did not promise that those

---

[4]See the discussion of this text, and what it does and does not mean, in chapter 1 above.

who had died [in the siege of Jerusalem] in 587 or those who would die during the exile itself, would literally come back to life to share in that return. . . .

Nevertheless, there is no doubt that Ezekiel's vision of the dry bones and their revival functions as a very important link in a theological chain to which the full biblical hope of resurrection is anchored. At one end is the connection we have already noted between Ezekiel's vision of God breathing life into the lifeless bodies of Israel's defunct army and the Genesis tradition of God breathing the breath of life into the human-shaped pile of dust that then became a living human being [Gen 2:7]. God's renewal of Israel was like a rerun of creation. Or, to put it the other way around, what God was about to do for Israel would be like the first act in the renewal of humanity as a whole. . . . Just as [Israel's] sin and punishment mirrored the fallenness of the whole human race, so too their restoration would prefigure God's gracious purpose of redemption for humanity. Resurrection for Israel anticipated resurrection for all.

And at the centre of the chain, of course, stands the risen Jesus himself. The most significant echo of Ezekiel 37 comes in a locked room on the very evening of his resurrection, when, we read, '[Jesus] breathed on them and said, "Receive the Holy Spirit."' [Jn 20:22]. The Lord of life himself, freshly risen to his feet from where he had lain among the bones of the dead,[5] adopts simultaneously the posture of Ezekiel in summoning the breath of God, and the posture of God himself in commanding the breath of the Spirit to come upon the disciples.

---

[5]I am speaking figuratively here of the tomb in general as the place of dry bones; we know that Jesus was laid in a new tomb in which nobody had previously been interred.

But this risen Jesus was the Messiah. And slowly the disciples came to realize that in the resurrection of the Messiah God had done, through Jesus, what they were hoping and expecting that God would do for Israel [Lk 24:19-27, 45-49]. The redemption, revival and resurrection of Israel were embodied in the resurrection of Jesus the Messiah. As James would later affirm, the Davidic monarchy was also restored [Acts 15:16-17], and as Hebrews would argue in detail, all the great realities of Israel's faith and covenantal security are now embodied in Jesus and inherited by those who believe in him—believing Jews and Gentiles alike.

So the resurrection of Jesus *did* fulfil the vision of Ezekiel through [Christ's] personal embodiment of the restoration of Israel. But, in line with the thrust of our earlier point, the restoration of Israel through Jesus was also the first stage of God's wider project of the redemption of the human race. The breath that breathed life into the dead came from *the four winds*—that is, from the Spirit of God who is at work everywhere in the world, in all directions. That which was focused with tremendous resurrection power on Ezekiel's dead bodies, and then on the dead Messiah, is the same power that is available to the ends of the earth to bring life, salvation and the hope of bodily resurrection to all who trust in the one who sends it. For 'if the Spirit of him who raised Jesus from the dead is living in you, he who raised Christ from the dead will also give life to your mortal bodies through his Spirit, who lives in you' (Rom 8:11).[6]

Once again, then, we find that the great teachings, prophecies and pictures of the Old Testament about the Spirit enrich our per-

---

[6]Wright, *Message of Ezekiel*, pp. 306-11.

sonal experience of life in Christ. Of course we say that we believe in the Holy Spirit. But, as we have seen from the very first chapter of this book, are we fully aware of all that he is, of all he has done, still does and will do? He is the Spirit of the God who spoke creation into existence and breathed life into humanity. He is the Spirit whom Ezekiel saw raising God's people from the dead. He is the Spirit who raised Jesus from the dead. He is the Spirit who now gives life to his people and to every individual in whom he dwells by faith in Christ. This—we gasp when we realize—is none other than "the Spirit who lives in you."

REPENTANCE AND RESTORATION: JOEL 2

At last we come to the passage which some people might have expected us to tackle right at the start of our study since it is the Old Testament text quoted by Peter on the day of Pentecost. And for some people (though not readers of this book by now), that is about all they know of the Holy Spirit in the Old Testament—namely that Joel foretold that the Spirit would be poured out, and since that happened at Pentecost, what more needs to be said?

And afterward,
    I will pour out my Spirit on all people.
Your sons and daughters will prophesy,
    your old men will dream dreams,
    your young men will see visions.
Even on my servants, both men and women,
    I will pour out my Spirit in those days.
I will show wonders in the heavens
    and on the earth,
    blood and fire and billows of smoke.

The sun will be turned to darkness
  and the moon to blood
  before the coming of the great and dreadful day of the LORD.
And everyone who calls
  on the name of the LORD will be saved;
for on Mount Zion and in Jerusalem
  there will be deliverance,
    as the LORD has said,
among the survivors
  whom the LORD calls. (Joel 2:28-32)

As always, we need to set this text in its wider context in the book of Joel, and especially in the remarkable second chapter.

Joel prophesied in the midst of a national disaster which he sees as the judgment of God. It is described as an invasion of locusts in Joel 1, and either it was simply that (locust invasions were, and still are, utterly devastating) or it was an invasion by some enemy army that is described metaphorically in this way. Most likely, it was in fact a plague of locusts. Joel 2 continues this theme for its first eleven verses. These verses are a mixture of simple description and frightening images, which those who have ever witnessed a locust attack say is very accurate. There is the devouring devastation (Joel 2:3), their frightening appearance and noise (Joel 2:4-5), the panic they cause (Joel 2:6), their invasion of cities and even houses (Joel 2:7-9), the way they make the ground seem to shiver and ripple and the sky turn dark (Joel 2:10).

But Joel mixes with these literal descriptions some other phrases that see behind it all the judgment of God. This is the "day of the LORD" (Joel 2:1, 11); it is like the fall of humanity in the garden of Eden (Joel 2:3); it is like the earthquake and darkness that symbolize the dread presence of God's wrath (Joel 2:10). And finally, quite explicitly, the army of locusts is nothing less than the LORD's own army, with him at the head—utterly frightening stuff.

> The LORD thunders
>   at the head of his army;
> his forces are beyond number,
>   and mighty are those who obey his command.
> The day of the LORD is great;
>   it is dreadful.
>   Who can endure it? (Joel 2:11)

But then suddenly and surprisingly, there is a complete change of tone at Joel 2:12. The God who is at the head of the devouring army of locusts in Joel 2:11 suddenly appeals to the people in the next verse to turn to him in repentance, "even now."

> "Even now," declares the LORD, "return to me with all your heart, with fasting and weeping and mourning."

Joel then jumps into the space created by what God has just said in Joel 2:12, with some added motivation and reasons to do what God says (Joel 2:13-14), with some practical instructions (Joel 2:15-17a) and with a ready-made liturgy of repentance (Joel 2:17b).

This, then, is the context that is leading us on eventually to the great promise of the outpouring of the Spirit later in the chapter. Before we get there, however, we need to see what this chapter says about genuine repentance and total forgiveness. For only then will we appreciate its promise of universal blessing. This, after all, was how Peter applied it on the day of Pentecost. On that occasion, Peter called for repentance and promised forgiveness and blessing to all who would respond to the outpouring of the Spirit and the message about Jesus. Peter himself knew the Holy Spirit through the Old Testament, so we must follow his example. Let's look, then, at what Joel has to say about repentance and forgiveness, to prepare ourselves for what he says about the coming of the Spirit.

Genuine repentance (Joel 2:12-17). How can we tell that the repentance described in these verses is genuine? Fundamentally because it is based upon *truth*. The motivation, the methods, and even the format, of the repentance Joel calls for are all founded on essential biblical truths about God and about God's people. At least three great realities stand out in these verses:

1. *God's grace (Joel 2:13)*
   Rend your heart
       and not your garments.
   Return to the LORD your God,
       for he is gracious and compassionate,
   slow to anger and abounding in love,
       and he relents from sending calamity.

The last three lines of this wonderful verse are like a refrain in the Old Testament. In fact, they are God's name-badge. It is God's own self-description when Moses asked to know his identity. This is who Yahweh is. This is the personal character that is to be understood every time that name is used. It comes for the first time in Exodus 34:6, and remarkably, there also it is in the context of terrible sin and the threat of total destruction. But (as we saw in chapter 2) because of the selfless intercession of Moses, God's wrath was averted and his amazing grace and forgiveness were demonstrated. From then on, the phrases of this great self-affirmation by God echo through the Old Testament at least eight times. You can check it out (it will make an encouraging read) in Numbers 14:18; Nehemiah 9:17; Psalm 86:15; 103:8; 145:8; Jonah 4:2; Nahum 1:3; and of course here in Joel 2:13.

In fact, these phrases (the last three lines of Joel 2:13) are the nearest the Old Testament comes to what we might call "propositional theology"—that is, defining the attributes of God. Deuteronomy 6:4 would be another such text—categorically affirming that the LORD God is one. These verses define that one God as fundamentally the God of grace and compassion.

But how can we cope with putting Joel 2:11 (God's anger) and Joel 2:13 (God's grace) together? They are both affirmed. And of course Israel knew Yahweh as the God of wrath against all human wickedness, pride and idolatry. But they also knew that this same God was the God of grace, of infinite love and mercy, who longed for nothing more than to have sinners turn to him in repentance so that he could meet them with mercy and blessing. For of course Joel 2:11 and Joel 2:13 do not actually stand together. Joel 2:12 comes in between, and what makes the difference is genuine repentance. Ultimately, we can hold these great Old Testament truths together only at the foot of the cross. For there we see the total outpouring of God's judgment alongside the ultimate demonstration of God's grace, as the wrath of God was borne by God himself in the willing person of his own Son.

2. God's covenant (Joel 2:17a)

"Return to the LORD *your God*," urges Joel 2:13. "Spare *your people*, O LORD," prays Joel 2:17. This is the language of the covenant relationship in which God had repeatedly said, "I will be your God and you will be my people." It is amplified by the phrase "your inheritance," also in Joel 2:17—which could refer to the people or the land or both together.

So here is repentance which appeals to the great fact of the covenant relationship between God and his people in the Old Testament. The people of Israel at that time were God's people in God's land, and God had made his commitment to them (as they had to him, of course, and then broken it). So they appeal to God not to break his commitment, not to destroy them, but rather to remember his own promises. The Israelites had been unfaithful to God, but they appeal to God to be faithful to himself. That is a firm foundation for all prayer, but especially repentance.

This is exactly the basis on which Moses, as we saw, appealed to God to spare the Israelites after the great apostasy of the golden calf in Exodus 32—34, which we considered in chapter two above. We looked at the prayer of Moses as he recalls it in Deuteronomy 9:25-29. It would be worth reading that prayer again and comparing it with what Joel puts in the mouths of the people here. In fact, you will find that this appeal to God's covenant marks all the great prayers of repentance and intercession in the Old Testament. Perhaps the most notable are those of Moses, Nehemiah and Daniel, respectively recorded in Deuteronomy 9, Nehemiah 9 and Daniel 9. That makes it easy to remember. Dial 999 for repentance and intercession.

3. *God's honor (Joel 2:17b)*

If God's people suffer shame and disgrace, then so does the God they call their own. The watching nations would not only mock Israel, they would jeer at Israel's God as well. "Where is their God?" they will taunt. And so, in their repentance and appeal to God to be merciful to them, they make this point to God. Is this what he wants to see happen? How can God allow his honor and glory to be trampled on and ridiculed in the world? Remember Moses saying to God, "What will the Egyptians think if you destroy these people in the wilderness after delivering them out of slavery?"

One of the marks of genuine repentance is that you find yourself more concerned for God's honor than your own. Coming to an awareness of your own sin can (should) produce deep shame. That is especially so if it is the kind of sin that involves other people and can bring embarrassment at the very least and complete ruin of one's reputation at the worst. But what makes it far worse is when you suddenly realize: "I am a Christian. I bear the name of Christ. What I have done is a disgrace to *his* name, not just mine. What damage this is doing, or could do, to the honor of the Lord and the good name of his people." At that point, you begin to cry out to the Lord, "Lord, have mercy. Spare me and forgive me, please, but do it not just for my sake, but for the sake of *your* name. I can't bear the thought of what people will say about you and all the others who carry your name. Lord, protect the honor of your own name. Don't let *my* sin and folly be the cause of mockery and slander against *you*." In that realization lays evidence of the work of the Holy Spirit.

Here then are the foundations for real prayer, and genuine repentance that moves the heart of God. These foundations are simple, but massive, biblical truths: God's identity and character is to be gracious; God is committed to his covenant promises; God's greatest concern is for the glory of his own name in the world. So when we are turning to God in repentance, or seeking to lead others to do so, let's get to the heart of God. Let our focus be not on my need, my fears and my reputation, but on God's character, God's covenant and God's honor. Then we can turn the "may" of Joel 2:14 into a confident, "He will turn . . ."

Total forgiveness (Joel 2:18-27). Try to imagine the scene. A massive act of national repentance is taking place, publicly announced (Joel 2:15), supported by every level of society (Joel 2:16), and led by

the religious leaders (Joel 2:17). That is what Joel calls for, and what
may well have happened.

At the end of Joel 2:17 there is silence. Waiting for God. The words
of scorn put into the mouths of the nations—"Where is their
God?"—are echoed as words of longing in the hearts of the people,
"Where is our God? What is his reply?" When you need a word from
the Lord, you need a prophet, and that is where Joel once again steps
into the situation with exactly that. He has a word from God, and it
is almost beyond belief. The God who was thundering in judgment
(Joel 2:11), now speaks words of utterly incredible grace and mercy,
beginning with the one they most needed to hear: "the LORD will . . .
take pity on his people" (Joel 2:18).

The message that follows in Joel 2:19-27 is one of immediate and
total forgiveness, demonstrated in restoration and blessing. The grace
they had appealed to in Joel 2:13 will now pour itself out in overwhelming physical beneficence. Take a moment to read and savor
those verses, remembering that you are hearing them in the context
of a devastating plague of locusts that has brought the whole land and
its agricultural survival to the brink of extinction. Here are just the
opening and closing notes.

> Then the LORD will be jealous for his land
>   and take pity on his people.
> The LORD will reply to them:
>   "I am sending you grain, new wine and oil,
>   enough to satisfy you fully;
> never again will I make you
>   an object of scorn to the nations." . . .
>
> You will have plenty to eat,
>   until you are full,

and you will praise the name
   of the LORD your God,
who has worked wonders for you;
   never again will my people be shamed.
Then you will know that I am in Israel,
   that I am the LORD your God,
   and that there is no other;
never again will my people be shamed. (Joel 2:19, 26-27)

What stands out in this joyful passage, as much as in the description of the people's repentance in Joel 2:12-17, are the same three elements: God's covenant, God's grace and God's honor, though with the strongest emphasis undoubtedly on the central one—grace.

1. *God's covenant*

We find here the same possessive relationships that were central to the covenant between God and Israel. They frame the whole section: "his land . . . his people" in Joel 2:18; "your God . . . my people" in Joel 2:27. That is the only framework for the saving work of God and experience of his mercy and forgiveness.

2. *God's grace*

God promises to restore all the damage done by the locusts, to give fresh growth and abundant harvests once again. It is a vivid and beautiful picture of the end of the locust invasion (Joel 2:20), of lovely sweet rain (Joel 2:23), of greenery and fruit (Joel 2:22) and of an overflowing plenitude of the blessings of life—grain, wine and olive oil (Joel 2:24).

At a deeper level it resonates with the language of judgment lifted, the curse driven back and blessing released. So although the text describes a historical recovery from a particularly bad locust attack in ancient Israel, it speaks also with overtones of God's ultimate purposes for the redemption of creation. When we read the Old Testament, we need to remember that Israel was called for the sake of all nations and their land often stands as a microcosm for the whole earth. This being so, it is striking that the song of rejoicing in Joel 2:21-23 is so comprehensive in those who are summoned to respond to what God is doing.

> Be not afraid *O land;*
> be glad and rejoice.
> Surely the LORD has done great things.
> Be not afraid, *O wild animals,*
> For the open pastures are becoming green.
> The trees are bearing their fruit;
> the fig tree and the vine yield their riches.
> Be glad, *O people of Zion,*
> rejoice in the LORD your God,
> for he has given you
> the autumn rains in righteousness.
> He sends you abundant showers,
> both autumn and spring rains, as before.
> (Joel 2:21-23, my italics)

Land, animals and humans are all included in the effects of God's saving purpose. God's blessing is for his whole creation—a truth and a joyful anticipation that is of ecological relevance today. No wonder that on other occasions the worshippers of Israel orchestrated a massive ode to joy among the whole of creation in anticipation of God coming to put things right in his world. Set Psalm 96:11-13 alongside these words of Joel and you will see what I mean.

But for the people, the words of greatest comfort and purest grace must surely be Joel 2:25:

> I will repay you for the years the locusts have eaten—
> > the great locust and the young locust,
> the other locusts and the locust swarm—
> > my great army that I sent among you.

"Repay you"? What a startling way to make the point. The word is a technical word for legal compensation. It means to make good some loss you have caused somebody else to suffer. God is offering to pay Israel back for the damage caused—as if it was God's fault, as if he is taking the blame, as if he were the one in the wrong, as if he owed them anything. In fact, of course, as Joel and all the prophets made so clear, the fault lies with Israel and their congenital rebellion and wickedness. Here was a people who, as so often before, deserved nothing at the hand of God other than destruction, and he is the one offering to pay them compensation!

It is wonderful enough to know, negatively, that

> He [God] does not treat us as our sins deserve
> > or repay us according to our iniquities,

as Psalm 103:10 puts it (though only the cross reveals what it cost God himself to be able to act in this way). That is amazing grace in itself, and not one of us would be here writing or reading this if it were not true. But that God should repay us what we *don't* deserve, what we lost because of our own sin (which is what Joel is talking about)— that is an even more amazingly positive act of sheer grace. Indeed, putting the two together produces that classic twin definition of God's mercy and God's grace. God's mercy is God *not* giving us what we *do* deserve. God's grace is God *giving* us what we *do not* deserve.

This verse, Joel 2:25, has been a favorite of many people for generations—understandably so. It speaks of God's power to renew and restore what has been lost in the devastation of our sinfulness. God can turn waste and loss into profit and growth. We should be careful to remember, though, that "the locusts" of this promise were in fact the agents of God's own judgment. We are not talking here merely about the "slings and arrows of outrageous fortune"—the accidents and lost opportunities, the failures and regrets, that are part of our everyday lives. It is of course another part of biblical truth that God is active within all the circumstances of our lives, that "in all things God works for the good of those who love him," and that nothing can separate us from the love of God in Christ (Rom 8:28-39). But this verse in Joel holds out the transformative, redemptive power of God, even over those things that have been the mark of judgment.

Sin has consequences—in this life as well as in eternity. Sin devastates and destroys. It wastes and ruins. And not all those consequences can be undone in this life. The murder victim does not come back to life because the murderer becomes a Christian. The family wrecked by adultery and divorce is not necessarily restored when the adulterer comes to Christ. But, nevertheless, the testimony of many is not only that genuine repentance *purges* the past (as Ezekiel 18:21-22 so explicitly declares), but that God's grace can *redeem* the past, and often does so in stunning ways.

So there is a terribly serious and terribly attractive word here for Christians who may be tempted, as I once was, to go on living in a state of life, or in a relationship, or in habits of behavior that they know to be sinful and displeasing to God. Stay there and the locusts will do their vicious work, robbing your life of greenery—joy, growth and fruitfulness. But turn in genuine repentance to God and not only will you sink into the warm cleansing waters of his mercy and grace, but you will discover his power to restore even those things you may have feared you had lost forever. I write as one who, by God's mercy, has learned the profound and humbling truth of this in experience— even in the midst of a lifetime of personal Christian profession and public Christian ministry. How many more years will you let the locusts eat before you turn back to the Lord and prove his promise?

3. *God's honor*

God heard the prayer of his people, not just that they should be spared the dreadful judgment but also that he, God himself, should not be slandered among the nations. Rather, they should know who the true and living God really is. But that knowledge has to start with the people of Israel themselves. How can the world come to know who God is, if his own people do not acknowledge him as they ought? So the climax of Joel's word of promise to the waiting people comes in Joel 2:27:

> Then you will know that I am in Israel,
>> that I am the LORD your God,
>> and that there is no other;
> never again will my people be shamed.

As a result of God's saving action, things will be known about him. The living presence of the one and only unique God would be known and would be so visible that the people he lives among would have no need for shame. On the contrary, they will rejoice to be known as his as much as he will be pleased to be known as theirs.

A missional vision is implicit here, at least in principle. For when God is known in Israel, then ultimately the nations too will come to know him. That, after all, was the reason why God had called and created Israel in the first place—to be a light to the nations, to be the means through which he would reveal himself and his saving purpose to the ends of the earth. And so the goal of God's acts of judgment as well as his acts of redemption is that ultimately the whole world will know him.

And that is what leads us, finally, to the climax of the whole chapter, as Joel's vision broadens out beyond the removal of the immediate danger (the plague of locusts), and even beyond the prospect of rapid recovery of the national economy, to what it all points toward in God's ultimate purpose. "And afterward," Joel adds (Joel 2:28), not specifying a time or date, but indicating a future prospect. And that brings us back to our main theme—the coming Spirit. For what a coming it is that Joel now portrays! In the context of genuine repentance and total forgiveness, we are now ready to picture that outpouring of the Spirit of God that Peter affirms took place at Pentecost.

Universal blessing (Joel 2:28-32). "*You* will know," says Joel 2:27. And the echo of so many other texts of the Old Testament is "and *the nations* will know." But how? How will the knowledge of God be spread? The answer in this immediate context is, by the overwhelming communicating power of the Spirit of God being poured out on his people in such a way that the prophetic word will be on everyone's lips.

In the previous verses God promised to pour out rain—sweet irrigating rain on thirsty ground and on vegetation devastated and devoured by the locusts of his judgment. But now it is not just rain, but his own Spirit that God promises to pour out. And we now know something of what this Spirit of God would have meant to Old Testament believers. This is the Spirit who birthed and sustains all creation. This is the Spirit who equips people for craftsmanship and empowers them for leadership. This is the Spirit who inspired the prophets to speak the truth and stand for justice. This is the Spirit who anointed kings and who will anoint the coming righteous Servant-king. This is the Spirit God says he is going to pour out "on all people"!

In these verses Joel tells us that the coming of the Spirit will be marked by effects that are universal, cosmic and saving.

1. Universal

Remember the longing of Moses, possibly expressed with ironic weariness, "I wish that all the LORD's people were prophets and that the LORD would put his Spirit on them!" (Num 11:29)? "He will," answers Joel, "He will!" The outpouring of God's Spirit will make what must have seemed like a dream to Moses into a real possibility. The Spirit will be available for all.

> And afterward,
>   I will pour out my Spirit on all people.
> Your sons and daughters will prophesy,
>   your old men will dream dreams,
>   your young men will see visions.
> Even on my servants, both men and women,
>   I will pour out my Spirit in those days. (Joel 2:28-29)

We can't miss the note of universality in this outpouring, for Joel expands his initial phrase "all people" in three remarkable ways. It will be on men and women (sons *and* daughters). It will be on old and young. And it will even be on slaves, male and female. In other words, there will be no privileged distinctions among God's people as regards who gets the Spirit—no distinctions of gender, age or class. All will have equal access to sharing in the outpouring that is promised. There is something very similar here to what Paul affirms has taken place in Christ:

> There is neither Jew nor Greek, slave nor free, male nor female,
> for you are all one in Christ Jesus. (Gal 3:28)

And Paul says this in the same context as telling the Galatians that, as the spiritual seed of Abraham in Christ, they have also received the "promise of the Spirit" (Gal 3:14), the Spirit who witnesses in our hearts that we are children of God (Gal 4:6). And this is what Peter told his listeners on the day of Pentecost also.

2. *Cosmic*

But it is not just that the Spirit will have his effect horizontally on all people, at the human level. Joel goes on to use language that implies a cosmic effect.

> I will show wonders in the heavens
>   and on the earth,
>   blood and fire and billows of smoke.
> The sun will be turned to darkness
>   and the moon to blood
>   before the coming of the great and dreadful day of the LORD.
>   (Joel 2:30)

This is the kind of language that biblical writers used when they wanted to intensify the significance of some event they were describing or anticipating. Sometimes there may have been quite literal events that could be described in such terms—as for example the earthquake and apparently volcanic fire and smoke that terrified the Israelites at Mount Sinai. But more often this kind of language is intended figuratively as a way of expressing something that is, as we might say, "earth-shaking"—that is, of tremendous, or ultimate, power and effectiveness. The psalmists used it a lot (cf. Ps 18:7-15; 97:5). We still use such language in somewhat modified ways when we describe some political event as "cataclysmic," or some historical event or battle as "a watershed," or some serious threat as "facing the abyss."

So, on the one hand, Joel, speaking in familiar prophetic language, probably did not mean us to take his words literally, and Peter certainly did not. For if on the day of Pentecost Jerusalem had actually been filled with blood, fire and smoke in the midst of a combined solar and lunar eclipse, we can be sure that the crowds would have had more to get excited about than a bunch of jabbering disciples whom they thought were drunk.

Yet, on the other hand, we cannot just dismiss Joel's imagery as purely rhetorical exaggeration. First of all, we should remember that the creation itself did respond to the climactic events of the death and resurrection of Jesus. The sun was darkened in the final hours of his crucifixion, and the earth quaked to mark both his death and his resurrection. And second, we should remember that the whole Bible teaches that the redeeming work of God (including of course the outpouring of the Spirit) encompasses the whole cosmic order. Paul tells us that through the cross God will bring about the reconciliation of the whole creation ("all things . . . in heaven and on earth") to himself (Col 1:20). And the outpouring of the Spirit was, after the resurrection itself, the first anticipation of the new creation. A whole new world was born on Easter Sunday, and a whole new era of the outpoured Spirit began at Pentecost. And, as Peter recognized, these things were of cosmic importance. The whole creation is affected. That is why he could point to what seemed so puzzling to the onlookers (the manifestation of the Spirit on the disciples), and boldly make an equation between "this" event and "that" Scripture. "*This*," he says, "(though it may not look like it) is *that* which was spoken by the prophet Joel" (Acts 2:16)—and then goes on to quote our text in full. After that he tells the story of Jesus, climaxing with the cosmic affirmation of Jesus' resurrection and ascension:

> Exalted to the right hand of God, he has received from the Father the promised Holy Spirit and has poured out what you now see and hear (Acts 2:33).

Paul takes the same theology to its cosmic conclusion when he speaks of the whole creation straining forward to that full redemption that will include us and it together and of how the Spirit is given to us as the "firstfruits," or guarantee, of this grand prospect (Rom 8:18-24). Joel's language of "wonders in the heavens and on the earth" seems almost restrained by comparison.

3. *Salvation*

We reach at last the climactic words of this chapter, the climactic words of Joel's sermon and of Peter's, and what must also be the climax of this book:

> And everyone who calls
> > on the name of the LORD will be saved;
> for on Mount Zion and in Jerusalem
> > there will be deliverance,
> > as the LORD has said,
> among the survivors
> > whom the LORD calls. (Joel 2:32)

Could you ever imagine that a chapter that begins as this one does—with words of sheer terror—could end with words of such promise? Listen again to the words of "alarm" in Joel 2:1-2:

Let all who live in the land tremble,
    for the day of the LORD is coming.
It is close at hand—
    a day of darkness and gloom,
    a day of clouds and blackness.

The chapter ends with another reference to the day of the LORD (at the end of Joel 2:31), but this time it is transformed into a day of opportunity and hope. There is salvation for anyone who wants it—all they have to do is call on the name of the LORD. That is, they must turn to Yahweh in the genuine repentance that is based on his grace, his covenant and his honor, as was carefully laid down in Joel 2:12-17. And so in the astonishing transformation that we have witnessed in this chapter, Yahweh, the LORD God who is Judge and executioner from the start of the book of Joel right through until Joel 2:11, has become the LORD God who is Savior of all who call on his name.

Peter holds out this verse from Joel to the Jews from around the Mediterranean who had gathered in Jerusalem, offering them salvation literally in the place where it had once been promised by Joel and where it had now been accomplished by Jesus. They are those who can now not only call on God, but whom God is actually calling to himself (as the last line of Joel 2 puts it and Peter echoes in Acts 2:39). All that is required is true repentance and baptism in the name of Jesus, through whose death forgiveness of sins is now possible. And if they do those things, then "you will receive the gift of the Holy Spirit" (Acts 2:38).

Paul, however, goes further still, for he sees even more clearly the universal implications of all that God had said and done in Israel. The salvation offered to Israel was the salvation offered to the world. For it was for the world's sake that God had chosen Israel, just as it was for the world's sake that he had sent his only Son. So Paul affirms,

> If you confess with your mouth, "Jesus is Lord," and believe in
> your heart that God raised him from the dead, you will be
> saved. For it is with your heart that you believe and are justi-
> fied, and it is with your mouth that you confess and are saved.
> As the Scripture says, "Anyone who trusts in him will never be
> put to shame." For there is no difference between Jew and Gen-
> tile—the same Lord is Lord of all and richly blesses all who call
> on him, for "Everyone who calls on the name of the Lord will
> be saved." (Rom 10:9-13)

"The name of the Lord." Clearly, when Joel wrote these words, he
meant the name of the LORD, Yahweh the God of Israel. Equally
clearly, when Paul quotes them, he means the Lord Jesus, for he has
just said that confessing "Jesus is Lord" is an essential criterion of salvation. In fact it was the earliest and shortest Christian creed. So we
have here one of the many places in the New Testament where words
of the Old Testament written by or about Yahweh, the God of Israel,
are calmly taken up and used about Jesus of Nazareth. Jesus is indeed
Immanuel, God with us. Jesus shares the identity of the true and living God of Israel's faith and worship and hope.

But what will lead people to say such words—in their hearts and
on their lips? None other than the Holy Spirit of God. For it is the
Spirit, as Jesus said, who "will convict the world of guilt in regard to
sin and righteousness and judgment" (Jn 16:8). So it will be the Spirit
who will thus lead people to see their need of the salvation God offers
through Christ. And it is only through the Holy Spirit, as Paul said,
that anyone can come to confess, "Jesus is Lord" (1 Cor 12:3). Joel
would have thoroughly agreed.

CONCLUSION

When the Spirit came at Pentecost, then, he came with a great deal of expectation hanging on his coming. In this chapter we have seen how the prophets of Israel looked forward to transformation at every level when the Spirit would come, according to God's promise. There would be change at cosmic, ecological, international, moral, spiritual and personal levels. We have to acknowledge, in relation to all this, that there is an "already . . . but not yet" about the fulfilment of these Spirit prophecies, just as there is about the kingdom of God as preached and inaugurated by Jesus. The kingdom has come, but not yet in all its fullness. The Spirit has come, but not yet with all that was promised. What we do see, most certainly, is the work of the Spirit in drawing people to repentance, forgiveness and restoration, just as Joel (and indeed Jesus) said he would.

And so, as we disembark from our long voyage of discovery of the Spirit of God in the Scriptures, and especially the Old Testament, our final picture of him must be one of him doing his favorite work— leading people to salvation in Christ. Yes, we now have grasped something of the vast scale of the work of the Spirit of God—in creation, in empowerment, in prophecy, in anointing for mission, in new creation. Perhaps the Holy Spirit will no longer be the neglected person of the Trinity that we have allowed him to be before. Or perhaps we will have a far richer appreciation of his person and activity than the limited role we normally allow him in certain kinds of worship or times of "ministry." But most of all, because God is the saving Father, and because Jesus is the saving Son, we will rejoice to see the saving Spirit, sent by both Father and Son to point men and women, sons and daughters, old and young, to the one in whom alone they can be saved.

LANGHAM LITERATURE

All the royalties from this book have been irrevocably assigned to Langham Literature (formerly the Evangelical Literature Trust). Langham Literature is a program of the Langham Partnership International, founded by John Stott. Chris Wright is the International Ministries Director.

Langham Literature distributes evangelical books to pastors, theological students and seminary libraries in the Majority World, and fosters the writing and publishing of Christian literature in many regional languages.

For further information on Langham Literature, and the other programs of LPI, visit the website at www.langhampartnership.org. In the USA, the national member of the Langham Partnership International is John Stott Ministries. Visit the JSM website at www.johnstott.org.

ALSO AVAILABLE

Knowing Jesus Through the Old Testament

We cannot know Jesus without knowing his story. But the debate over who he is rages on. Has the Bible bound Christians to a narrow and mistaken notion of Jesus? Should we listen to other Gospels, other sayings of Jesus, that enlarge and correct a mistaken story? To answer these questions we need to know what story Jesus claimed for himself. Christopher Wright is convinced that Jesus' own story is rooted in the story of Israel. In *Knowing Jesus Through the Old Testament* he traces the life of Christ as it is illuminated by the Old Testament. And he describes God's design for Israel as it is fulfilled in the story of Jesus.